HOW TO REDUCE THE TAX YOU PAY

HOW TO REDUCE THE TAX YOU PAY

Planning through 1997,
Plus Tips for 1996 Returns

KEY PORTER BOOKS

Canadian Cataloguing in Publication Data

The National Library of Canada has catalogued this publication as follows:

Main entry under title:

How to reduce the tax you pay

[1988] –

Annual.

ISSN 1187-0028

ISBN 1-55013-820-0 (1996: Deloitte & Touche)

ISBN 1-55013-862-6 (1996: Samson Bélair/Deloitte & Touche)

1. Tax Planning – Canada – Periodicals.

2. Income tax – Canada.

I. Deloitte & Touche. II. Samson Bélair/Deloitte & Touche (Firm)

HJ4661.H68 343.7105'2'05 C91-090997-0

Key Porter Books Limited
70 The Esplanade
Toronto, Ontario
Canada M5E 1R2

Design/Electronic formatting: Heidi Palfrey

Printed and bound in Canada

96 97 98 99 00 6 5 4 3 2 1

The information and analysis contained in this book are not intended to substitute for competent professional advice. Planning your tax and financial affairs to reduce the tax you pay is a complex process – one that is unique to you or your business. The material that follows is provided solely as a general guide to assist you in understanding the main income tax provisions you can use to minimize your tax burden. No action should be initiated without consulting your professional advisors. This book reflects the law and legislative proposals to November 1, 1996.

How to Reduce the Tax You Pay was compiled by a team of writers from Deloitte & Touche and (in Quebec) Samson Bélair/Deloitte & Touche, serving Canadian clients for more than 135 years. The firm is one of the largest offering the services of chartered accountants and management consultants, with more than 4,100 people, including over 560 partners and over 3,100 professional staff in some 65 Canadian centres. We provide a full range of accounting and auditing, tax and management consulting services to more than 60,000 clients in all sectors of the Canadian economy. We are a leader in serving *The Financial Post*'s top 500 industrial companies, and audit more of the nation's top financial institutions than any other accounting firm.

As a member of Deloitte Touche Tohmatsu International, we serve multinational and large national enterprises, public institutions, and tens of thousands of fast-growing small businesses. We audit more than 700 companies with sales or assets in excess of US$1 billion. Numbering 59,000, our internationally experienced professionals in 124 countries deliver seamless, consistent services wherever our clients operate.

CO-EDITORS:

Paul Alliston, Toronto
Richard Wilson, Montreal

CONTRIBUTORS:

Gisèle Archambault, Montreal
Mario Bastonnais, Montreal
Marty Blatt, Edmonton
Pat Bouwers, Toronto
John Bowey, Kitchener
John Budd, Toronto
Peter Clayden, Vancouver
Sharon Forsey, St. John's
René Huot, Montreal
John Hutson, Kitchener
Anne Montgomery, Toronto
Keith Pitzel, Winnipeg
Len Sakamoto, Toronto
Bill Sherman, Toronto
Linda Stillabower, Toronto
Brian Taylor, Saskatoon

PRODUCTION SUPPORT:

Junia Fulgence, Toronto

Contents

Foreword

Do you want to pay more income tax than the law requires? Of course you don't – but that is exactly what many Canadians do, for several reasons. Some may fail to understand the tax rules, or how they are applied. Others miss out on tax planning opportunities that the law provides, or fail to take advantage of specific tax incentives that are readily available. Far too many taxpayers make errors in completing their tax returns, errors that the tax department may not be able to identify or correct. And finally, some people just can't seem to meet the deadlines imposed under the law, and therefore end up paying interest and penalties on top of what they owe.

We think this book can help you to avoid costly mistakes, and to reduce or defer your tax burden through intelligent planning – both for your 1996 return, and throughout 1997.

Tax Calendar[1]

December 31, 1996	Due date for single instalment of 1996 taxes for farmers and fishermen.
February 28, 1997	Last day for filing 1996 T4 and T5 summaries and sending slips to payees.
March 1, 1997	Last day for RRSP contributions eligible for deduction from 1996 personal income tax.
March 15, 1997	Due date for 1st quarterly instalment of 1997 personal income taxes.
April 15, 1997	Due date for 1996 U.S. personal income tax returns and last day for filing for extension.
April 30, 1997	Due date for filing 1996 personal income tax returns and for payment of balance of 1996 income taxes. Where a taxpayer died in 1996, terminal return due on the later of April 30, 1997, and six months following the date of death.
June 15, 1997	Due date for 2nd quarterly instalment of 1997 personal income taxes.
September 15, 1997	Due date for 3rd quarterly instalment of 1997 personal income taxes.
November, 1997	Good month for taking a final look at your tax planning for 1997.
December 15, 1997	Due date for 4th quarterly instalment of 1997 personal income taxes.
December 31, 1997	Due date for single instalment of 1997 taxes for farmers and fishermen.

[1] Remittances of amounts deducted or withheld are considered to be received on the date they are actually received and not the date they were mailed. Note that, if the payments are made at a chartered bank, they are considered to have been received by Revenue Canada at that time.

CHAPTER ONE

The Tax Planning Process

TAX PLANNING

No one should pay more tax than the law requires. The best way of not paying more than your fair share of taxes is through tax planning. Tax planning is not tax evasion. Tax evasion is any manoeuvre the purpose of which is to hide income otherwise subject to tax, for example, failing to declare all your interest income on your tax return. Tax planning involves reviewing your financial goals, and arranging your activities to achieve those goals at the least tax cost by using tax rules that permit you to reduce or defer taxation, increase deductions, or avoid tax traps.

"Loopholes"

Tax incentives are specially implemented by law to encourage certain activities. If you take advantage of such incentives, you are doing precisely what the government encouraged you and other taxpayers to do. These provisions are therefore the exact opposite of loopholes, which are inadvertent errors in the design and structure of the law.

Where to Begin

Usually, the first step in effective tax planning is to find out where you stand today. Chapter 13 contains statistical tables to help you determine your tax position for 1996. This will provide a starting point for computing the tax effect of the various proposals and plans set forth in this book. Other factors to consider in your planning include interest rates, projected inflation rates, current income tax rules, and the possibility of future legislative changes. Once you have considered all the factors relevant to your situation, you should be in a position to implement your tax plan.

Two concepts are fundamental to understanding how tax planning works. The first is the time value of money, which helps to explain tax deferral, and the second is marginal tax brackets.

KEY PLANNING CONCEPTS

Tax planning essentially involves five main activities:

- *income splitting* – transferring income from a taxpayer in a high tax bracket to one in a lower tax bracket;
- *income shifting* – transferring income from a high tax rate year to a lower rate year; conversely, shifting deductions from a low rate year to a high rate year;
- *investment selection* – transforming income from a fully taxed source to one that is eligible for full or partial exemption;
- *tax deferral* – delaying taxation of income;
- *tax shelters* – using tax law incentives to maximize deductions and minimize taxable income.

Time Value of Money

This concept essentially says that one dollar received today is worth more to us than the same dollar received in the future. For example, if we receive one dollar today, we can invest it to earn interest. After one year, we will have one dollar plus the interest income. If we had not received that dollar until the end of the year, we would have lost the opportunity to earn the interest. Similarly, paying one dollar in taxes today is more expensive than doing so in the future, as we lose the interest that dollar could have earned.

Tax Deferral

Postponing payment of taxes is tax deferral. One major aspect of tax planning involves deferring tax payments as long as possible. The longer we are able to do so, the longer our money remains available for investment and other activities.

Marginal Tax Brackets

As your taxable income increases, the percentage of tax that must be paid upon that income also increases. In other words, your upper-end income is more heavily taxed than your lower-end income. Different tax rates at different income levels result in marginal tax brackets, which tell us how much will be paid to the government in taxes from each additional dollar of taxable income we earn.

The concept of marginal tax brackets is a key aspect of family income planning, in particular, income splitting. For example, if the primary earner in the family is in a 45 per cent tax bracket and can transfer income to a family member in a 26 per cent bracket, the family will save 19 cents for every dollar of taxable income transferred (until that family member moves into the next tax bracket).

The marginal tax brackets also tell us how much we will save if we incur costs that are tax-deductible. If your marginal tax bracket is 45 per cent and you can deduct one dollar from that taxable income, it will save 45 cents in taxes; this 45-cent saving means that the actual after-tax cost of spending that tax-deductible dollar is 55 cents. Obviously, the concept of marginal tax brackets makes tax-deductible expenditures more valuable to high-income taxpayers than to low-income taxpayers.

Tax Credits versus Tax Deductions

A tax deduction decreases taxable income, and saves tax based on the marginal tax bracket. A tax credit, however, is an amount subtracted to arrive at the actual tax due. It is not part of the calculation of taxable income.

Thus, a tax credit of $100 will result in a tax saving of $100, regardless of the individual's marginal tax bracket. Conversely, a $100 expenditure that results in a tax deduction will save an individual in a 45 per cent bracket $45, but will save an individual in a 26 per cent bracket only $26.

TAX PLANNING GOALS

Your primary tax objective should be to recognize taxable income at the time, and in the form, in which it will be most favourably taxed.

Remember, it is unlikely that a particular tax incentive or tax plan can convert a bad investment into a good one.

Suppose an investment generates tax deductions of $100, resulting in a real tax saving of about $51. If you anticipate losing the full amount you invested, your real economic cost, after the tax saving, is 49 per cent of the cost. This is not smart tax planning, nor is it a "tax shelter". This is a foolish investment!

A Word on Tax Audits

The tax authorities have three years from the time your tax return is initially assessed to review the information and make any re-assessment of your taxes. Although there is an excellent chance that you never will be audited, it is important to be able to explain the information on your return if you are asked. Accordingly, one aspect of your financial and tax planning must be good recordkeeping. You need to document the intent and the details of your various transactions and all aspects of your business and financial activities. This documentation will assist you in remembering several years later exactly what occurred. Should the tax authorities decide to audit you, this detailed documentation will provide evidence of careful and businesslike planning, an important aspect of many areas of tax law.

There is no need to fear a tax audit if your tax plans are well designed and well documented in accordance with tax law. Conversely, if you have made misrepresentations through neglect, carelessness, or wilful default, or if you have committed fraud, you do have something to worry about! You also should note that there is no time limit for assessment on such activities!

GETTING STARTED

Tax planning is essentially a simple process with a few basic elements. It should be an integral part of your regular financial planning and budgeting process, since it is a year-round activity. Unless you have planned carefully throughout the year, your opportunities for reducing your tax bill become more and more restricted as the year end approaches. Tax planning can be most effective when begun immediately.

Get started!

CHAPTER TWO

Income and Deduction Basics

Since you are taxed differently, depending on the type of income earned, the first step in tax planning is to look at your sources of income. Three main categories of income are taxed: employment income, business income, and income from property and capital gains. Various other specific items of income may or may not be taxed. If you have received a benefit of any kind from any activity, it is likely to be taxable. Conversely, an expenditure generally is not deductible unless it is necessary to generate a type of taxable income.

EMPLOYMENT INCOME

You probably have the least opportunity for tax planning in relation to income from employment. Your taxable employment income in most cases will include any benefit you receive by virtue of that employment. Generally, these amounts are measured by your employer and reported to you and to the government on your T4 (Relevé 1 in Quebec) each year.

Fringe Benefits

Included in your taxable employment income are such things as personal use of an employer's auto, certain premiums paid by the employer under provincial hospitalization and medical-care plans, prizes and incentive awards, financial counselling, travel benefits, and the total cost of group life insurance. On the other hand, non-taxable benefits include such things as subsidized meals, uniforms or special clothing required for the job, recreational facilities provided at your work location, discounts on merchandise you purchase from your employer for personal use, retirement or re-employment counselling, mental or physical health counselling, and private health and income insurance plans.

Although there is less planning flexibility with employment income as compared with other sources of income, there are various compensation alternatives that may be available to you through your employer. A number of these have tax implications, as follows.

Employee Loans

The term "employee loan" is commonly used to describe any situation in which the employee may be taxed on any imputed interest benefit resulting from indebtedness to an employer. However, "employee loan" is a misnomer. The benefit rules apply not only to loans but to any other form of debt incurred by virtue of the previous, current, or future office or employment of an individual. It is not necessary that the employee be the debtor, nor is there any requirement that the employer be the creditor. For example, the imputed interest rules will apply if the employer makes a loan to the employee's child to help support his or her university education, or if an employee obtains a bank loan at a below-market interest rate due to the employer's involvement. Regardless of the actual debtor, any imputed interest benefit will be taxable in the hands of the employee. The rules also apply to third-party loans where the employer is financing part or all of the cost of the loan.

The amount of the taxable benefit to be included in income is generally calculated as the difference between interest that would be paid using the prevailing prescribed interest rate, set by the government each quarter, and interest actually paid within the year or 30 days after the end of the calendar year.

For example, if you borrow $10,000 from your employer at 2 per cent and the prescribed rate is 8 per cent all year, you must include $600 in income as a taxable benefit (8 per cent minus 2 per cent times $10,000), assuming the loan is outstanding for the entire year.

Commercial Rate Rule. The taxable benefit rules do not apply to an employee loan on which interest is charged at a rate equal to or above the commercial lending rate, having regard to all the terms and conditions of the loan, available at the time the loan was made.

Home Purchase Loans. A home purchase loan is a loan made to enable the borrower or a related person to acquire a dwelling to be inhabited by him or her, or to refinance a mortgage on such a dwelling. The definition includes a loan used to acquire a share of a co-operative housing corporation entitling the purchaser or a related person to inhabit a dwelling unit owned by such corporation.

The taxable benefit on home purchase loans is determined using the lesser of the prescribed rate of interest for the current period and the prescribed rate at the time the loan was made. (The prescribed rate for this purpose for 1996 was 7 per cent for the first quarter of the year, 6 per cent for the second quarter, and 5 per cent for the balance of the year.) All home purchase loans are considered to have a term not exceeding five years, so that, on each fifth anniversary date of the loan, a new loan is deemed to be received, and the prescribed rate of interest at that time applies for the next five-year period.

Because of the way the prescribed rate is calculated, we know in advance what the rate will be in the following quarter. This provides a planning opportunity. An employee who is arranging a loan from his or her employer to acquire (or to repay a loan that had been used to acquire) a home should consider requesting a short-term loan initially (i.e., less than three months). If the prescribed rate for the next quarter is lower than (or the same as) the current quarter, another short-term loan can be arranged. If the prescribed rate is showing a tendency to rise over an extended period, a long-term (e.g., five-year) loan could be finalized in the current quarter.

Home Relocation Loans. When an employee relocates or takes up a new position after May 23, 1985, is eligible to claim moving expenses, and has received a low-interest or interest-free loan to assist with the acquisition of a home at the new location, he or she will be able to deduct a specified amount of the taxable benefit relating to this home purchase loan in arriving at taxable income. The deduction is equal to the lesser of the actual benefit included in income and the benefit from a $25,000 interest-free employee loan. This deduction will be available for the lesser of five years or the length of time the home purchase loan (or a replacement loan for it) is outstanding. In general, moving expenses may be claimed if the employee's new residence is at least 40 kilometres closer to the new work location than his or her previous residence.

Deductibility of Imputed Interest. Employees may claim an offsetting deduction for any imputed interest included in income as a taxable benefit, provided such interest otherwise would be deductible if it were actually paid. For example, low-interest or interest-free loans used for investment purposes (including investment in shares of an employer corporation), or for the purchase of an automobile or aircraft used in the business of the employer, will be an extremely attractive perquisite of employment because the interest is deductible. (You will, of course, want to consider the tax treatment of automobiles used for business purposes, discussed in Chapter 9.)

Note, however, that any potential deduction is available only to the debtor, even though the interest benefit may be included in another taxpayer's (i.e., the employee's) income. Where there is a potential interest deduction, it is likely best to ensure that the employee is the debtor; otherwise the employee will have the taxable benefit but not the offsetting deduction. If, however, the debtor is in a higher tax bracket than the employee, it would be an advantage for the deduction to be in the hands of the debtor.

Benefits from Employee Loans. Interest-free or low-interest loans can produce a worthwhile benefit even if interest is imputed as a taxable benefit, since the tax on the imputed interest would always be less than the interest paid in the marketplace. Assuming that you borrow $25,000 from your employer at 6 per cent and otherwise would have to borrow at 8 per cent, you will save $500 each year in interest charges. No taxable benefit arises because the rate of interest you pay is higher than or equal to the prescribed rate (assuming that the prescribed rate does not exceed 6 per cent). Note that the interest would have to be paid by January 30 of the following year; otherwise it would not reduce the imputed benefit.

Of course, the benefits are even greater if the employee loan is interest-free. If your marginal rate of tax is 44 per cent and you borrow $25,000, your cost of the loan is the tax paid on the imputed benefit of $1,500 ($25,000 at 6 per cent), which is $660 (assuming the prescribed rate is 6 per cent throughout the year and the loan is outstanding for a full year). This works out to an effective interest charge of 2.64 per cent and a saving of $1,340, compared with the 8 per cent loan ($2,000 minus $660). If the loan is used to earn investment income, the imputed interest of $1,500 is deductible and there is no cost associated with the loan, whereas your after-tax cost on a conventional loan would be $1,120 ($2,000 less tax saving at 44 per cent).

Shareholder Loans. If you are a shareholder as well as an employee, you must consider special rules regarding loans or advances from your company. Although many of the rules for low-interest and interest-free loans are the same, there are greater tax implications regarding the granting of such loans. See Chapter 3.

Deferred Income Plans. Employers frequently offer such plans, many of which involve retirement planning. Whether tax is deferred on employment income depends on the nature of your particular plan. See Chapters 3 and 6.

Employee Stock Options

The tax rules relating to stock options are extremely complex. To avoid any nasty tax surprises, it would be best to obtain professional advice on this subject.

Expenses Connected with Employment

Generally, employees are not entitled to claim deductions for expenditures they incur as a result of their employment, unless such deductions are specifically authorized in the Income Tax Act. Employment expenses that may be deductible include union or professional dues (not including the initiation fee), automobile expenses, moving expenses, supplies consumed in the performance of one's duties, if required by contract to pay for them, and legal expenses incurred to collect or establish a right to salary or wages owing by an employer. Special expense deduction provisions exist for clergy, travelling salespeople, musicians, artists, and certain railway and transport employees. If you qualify, be sure you have the appropriate prescribed forms signed by your employer.

Legal expenses paid after 1985 to collect or establish a right to a retiring allowance (which includes rewards for wrongful dismissal) or pension benefit are deductible. The deduction is limited to the amounts received that are not transferred to an RRSP or RPP. Excess amounts can be carried forward for deduction in any of the seven following years. Any reimbursement of these fees must be included in income.

An individual certified as having a severe and prolonged impairment may deduct, to a maximum of $5,000, the costs of care provided by a part-time adult attendant who is not the individual's spouse. The deduction is limited to two-thirds of eligible income, which includes income from employment or self-employment, a training allowance, or a grant for research or similar work (net of expenses). This deduction is in addition to the personal tax credit that may be claimed by such a certified person. See Chapter 5.

Automobile Expenses

If you use your own automobile for your employer's business, or in your own business, you may be entitled to deduct automobile expenses. See Chapter 9.

Moving Expenses

Moving expenses are deductible if you meet certain conditions and the expenses are not reimbursed by your employer. The moving expenses must be incurred in beginning a business, employment, or full-time post-secondary education at a new location. The distance between your old residence and your new work or school location must be at least 40 kilometres greater than the distance between your new residence and your new work or school location.

Qualifying expenditures include the travelling costs to move you, your family, and your household goods, as well as meals and lodging en route, disposal costs in respect of your old residence, and legal services in respect of the purchase of the new residence, provided you or your spouse sold your old residence. You also may deduct storage costs for your household goods incurred in the course of the move. There are limits on the total amount that will be deductible, depending on the particular circumstances of your move.

BUSINESS INCOME

Income from Business or Property

If an activity is a business, you generally are taxed on the "profit" from that business, as measured by the revenue generated minus the expenses incurred in generating the revenue. If you realize a loss on the activity, this loss may offset income from employment, investment income, and so forth. (If the losses are generated from farming, their availability to offset other types of income, including income from other businesses, is restricted in certain circumstances.)

If the activity gives rise to income from the disposition of property, either the income will be fully included in calculating taxable income, or it will be a capital gain, eligible for a partial exclusion.

The economic reality of the activity should control its tax treatment. However, it is absolutely critical that you have detailed documentation of your activity. If you are starting a new business while you remain employed, you must maintain detailed records to demonstrate that you have a reasonable expectation of profit from the business, and that you are approaching the business in a professional manner. This includes obtaining businesslike advice, if necessary, and demonstrating that you either have abilities in the field or are seeking guidance. If you cannot demonstrate an expectation of profit and a businesslike approach to the activity, you may be treated as having a hobby. If so, your tax deductions will be restricted to the income generated from the activity. If the activity generates a loss, you will not be able to offset the loss against other income. Maintaining such records is particularly important for any activity, including farming, which is done on a part-time basis. If your activity generates losses for a number of years, the tax authorities are strongly inclined to view it as a hobby rather than a business.

Conversely, if you have entered into the activity as an investment, hoping to use the property acquired to generate income, it is equally important that you document this intent and provide evidence that it is reasonable to expect that the property will give rise to investment income. For example, if you buy a piece of land, expecting to build an office building or some other income-generating asset, the land may be a capital asset eligible for capital gains treatment on disposition. If, on the other hand, you invest in land with the intention of holding it to generate income from its rise in value, this would probably be considered an adventure in the nature of trade, or a business (depending on the volume of similar activity), and would probably result in fully taxable income. (The tax authorities are more inclined to treat increases in value as ordinary income and decreases in value as capital than they are to treat increases as capital and decreases as ordinary income.)

Taxation of Income from a Business

Generally, there are more opportunities for tax planning if you are self-employed or own a business than there are for employees. Different tax rules apply to business income. In addition, taxation of income from your business will differ, depending upon whether the business is operated in corporate or unincorporated form. (See Chapter 8 for a discussion of the advantages and disadvantages of incorporation, as well as a number of aspects of tax planning for small businesses.) Note that you may transfer assets from an unincorporated business to a partnership or a corporation on a tax-deferred basis, subject to certain restrictions.

Generally, you will be taxed on the "profit" from your business, regardless of how much you withdraw from the business (assuming your business is unincorporated). Profit is measured by deducting from the gross income of the business various expenses that are allowed as deductions. These expenses must be reasonable in amount and must be incurred for the purpose of generating income. Common deductions include the cost of merchandise sold, and expenditures for salaries, supplies, rent, advertising, and so forth. The amounts spent for enduring items such as furniture or equipment are not deductible, but you may claim capital cost allowances (depreciation) for such acquisitions.

Except for farming and fishing, profit is determined on an accrual basis, rather than on a cash basis.

Home Office Expenses

If you are self-employed or run your own sideline business and have an office in your home, you may be able to deduct expenses relating to that office.

For home office expenses to be deductible, the office must be either your principal place of business, or must be used exclusively to earn business income and be used on a regular and continuous basis for meeting clients, customers, or patients.

The amount deducted cannot exceed the income from the business for the year, after other expenses are deducted. Any excess amount may be carried forward to be deducted in years when the business generates income. In Quebec, for taxation years beginning after May 9, 1996, home office expenses are limited to 50 per cent of the amount that would otherwise be deductible.

Taxation Year

The 1995 federal budget mandated a December 31 fiscal year end for unincorporated businesses, with transitional relief for those businesses that, as a result, would have had two year ends in 1995. However, except for certain professional partnerships, an unincorporated business may have any year end, but it must adjust its income from the business to a calendar year for tax purposes. Individuals and eligible partnerships that initially adopt an off-calendar fiscal year end are permitted to change to a December 31 fiscal year end for a taxation year, provided notification is made before the filing deadline for the individuals' or partners' income tax returns for the year of the change. However, once a business of an individual or eligible partnership has adopted a December 31 fiscal year end, it is not subsequently allowed to change to an off-calendar fiscal year end.

PROPERTY INCOME AND CAPITAL GAINS

The third major income category is income from property, including interest, dividends, and rent. Capital gains are connected with property income, but are subject to special rules for the taxable amounts. See Chapter 7.

Gains from transfers of property (sales, gifts, etc.), including gains from sales of property used solely for personal purposes, generally are taxable. The primary exceptions to this rule are certain tax-deferred transfers between spouses, certain transfers of farm property to children, and gains from the sale of a personal residence if it is designated as your principal residence (see below). Transfers between spouses and others are discussed in Chapter 4.

Deductible Interest

If you borrow funds and the funds are used to earn income, any interest expense incurred is deductible from income, with certain exceptions. Earning income does not necessarily mean that you have to earn a profit immediately. There only need be a reasonable expectation of profit; therefore, incurring a loss does not prejudice the deductibility of the interest expense. However, the tax authorities may disallow the portion of the interest expense that exceeds the return on your investment if it was reasonably foreseeable, at the time the loan was taken out, that the rate of interest would exceed the rate of return in the future.

Before 1994, interest expense was deductible only if you

continued to own the related investment throughout the period of time the funds were borrowed. For example, if you borrowed $1,000 to purchase shares, but you sold the shares after only two months, interest for the period after the date of sale was not deductible. If you sold the shares for $400 and purchased other stock immediately for this amount, a portion of the interest ($400/$1,000) would then be deductible. You could not deduct the portion of the interest related to the loss realized on the sale of the shares. Since 1994, however, special rules have permitted the deduction of interest, after the property is sold, on that portion of the loan represented by the loss.

You are never allowed to deduct the interest on funds borrowed for personal expenditures, such as interest on money borrowed to finance a vacation or purchase a home. Thus, you should attempt to borrow only for investment or business purposes and pay for personal expenditures out of your savings. However, you are permitted to deduct interest when a personal asset (such as your home) has been used as collateral for a loan to finance an investment.

Principal Residence

You will not be taxed on the gain on disposition of a residence if you meet the principal residence exemption rules. Only the ownership interest in one home can be designated as your principal residence for a particular year. You can make the designation only for years you are resident in Canada. In addition, for years after 1981, only one principal residence per family unit per year is allowed, rather than the one unit per person per year that was allowed prior to 1982.

A house, condominium, mobile home, trailer, houseboat, or a share in a cooperative housing corporation qualifies. It can be owned outright, or jointly with one or more other individuals. In addition, it does not have to be located in Canada in order to qualify. (Tax might be payable in the other country on the disposition.)

For the home to be your principal residence, you, your spouse, or your child must be ordinarily resident in the home during the designated year. Usually the family home is designated, but a part-time residence, such as a summer cottage, can qualify. If you have more than one family home and must decide which home to designate and for how many years, the decision can be quite complex. Consider consulting your professional advisor prior to the sale.

Post-1981 Principal Residence Rules. Beginning in 1982, a family unit is able to designate only one home under the principal residence rules with respect to each year. In any particular year, a family unit consists of you, your spouse (provided you had a spouse throughout the year and were not throughout the year living apart and legally separated), and children who were throughout the year unmarried and under 18 years of age. This means that if you and your spouse each own a home, you will be liable for tax on all or a portion of the capital gain accruing on one of the homes beginning January 1, 1982. This gain was eligible for the former $100,000 capital gains exemption and the related special election in your 1994 income tax return, for gains accrued to February 29, 1992. If you did not make the election, you may still find it beneficial to do so, though you will have to pay a late-filing penalty. See Chapter 7. When a couple marries after 1981 and each owns a home, each may designate his or her home for the year of marriage and prior years, but only one home may be designated after the year of marriage. (Note that common-law couples are treated the same as married couples for 1993 and subsequent taxation years.)

Determining the Taxable Portion. The taxable portion of the gain on the sale of a principal residence is determined by subtracting the exempt portion from the total gain. The remainder, if any, is subject to normal capital gains rules (three-fourths included in income, but possibly eligible for the lifetime capital gains exemption, by way of a late-filed election, to the extent the gain was earned prior to March 1, 1992).

The exempt portion is based on the number of years that the property was a principal residence compared with the number of years of ownership. The actual rules are complicated. However, if you can designate the property as your principal residence for all years of ownership, or all years except one, the total gain is generally exempt.

Special transitional rules apply where a property owned on December 31, 1981, is subsequently sold. The rules provide that the non-exempt portion of the gain is the lesser of two amounts. Both amounts are calculated on the basis outlined above. One calculation is done by viewing the total years of ownership as one period (i.e., the normal method) and the other calculation is done by separating the years of ownership into two periods, one pre-1982 and one post-1981. To do this latter calculation, the fair market value of the property on December 31, 1981, must be determined.

Designating a Property as a Principal Residence. If, during the year, you dispose of a property that you wish to claim as your principal residence, and a portion of the gain is subject to tax, you must file a prescribed form with your tax return for that year, designating it as your principal residence for the years chosen. If the gain is completely exempt from tax, the tax authorities do not require the form to be filed.

Planning. If your family currently has, or intends to acquire, a second home, record all capital costs associated with your homes. These would include the costs of adding a pool, finishing the basement, or adding an extra room. Unless a record is kept of such expenditures, you may have to compute any ultimate gain using the original purchase price as the cost base of the property, which may be much lower than the total invested in the property.

In addition, if the family has only one house, consider transferring the ownership of the personal residence to the lower-income spouse. See Chapter 4.

To Sell or Not to Sell. Consider retaining your residence if you are leaving on an indefinite or temporary basis. During your absence, you may rent your home and still retain your ability to designate it as your principal residence for the years in which you were living there and, provided certain conditions are met, for up to four years after that. In addition, during the years of rental, you may deduct various costs and expenses. If you sell the residence instead of reoccupying it, the gain that accrued during years in which you designate the home as a principal residence will be tax-free. The gain that accrued during years when the residence was rented may not be taxable if the rental period was less than five years.

Special rules will extend the four-year maximum period referred to above if the housing unit is not occupied as a result of your employer or your spouse's employer requiring that you or your spouse relocate. Certain conditions must be met to take advantage of this extension.

Other special rules apply if a housing unit was originally acquired as a principal residence and was later used to earn rental or business income on a permanent basis (or vice versa). The rules defer the recognition of the resulting capital gain until disposition of the housing unit.

Rental Expenses

If you own investment property and earn rental income, you may deduct all the current expenses you incur with respect to the rental property and claim capital cost allowance (CCA) on the property itself.

However, CCA cannot be used to create or increase a loss with respect to rental property. It can offset only the net rental income on that, or other, property prior to the CCA claim.

Current expenses include the cost of advertising for tenants, heat, electricity, property taxes, water rates, insurance, and labour and material for routine repairs and maintenance. Capital expenditures such as major additions or renovations are not deductible, but can usually be added to the capital cost of the property and then claimed more slowly as CCA.

If you rent out part of your principal residence, the same basic rules apply for current expenses. Expenses fully attributable to the rented portion are fully deductible. Common expenses such as heat, electricity, and property taxes must be prorated so that only the portion that relates to the rented part of the principal residence is deducted from rental income. You may claim CCA for the rented portion, but you may not want to take this deduction because doing so will erode part of your principal residence exemption and cause a portion of any gain on a subsequent sale to be taxable.

If you are designating your house as a principal residence for years during which you are not occupying it, you cannot claim CCA on it for those years.

OTHER INCOME

Income from sources other than employment, business, or property is probably taxable. If in doubt, seek professional advice.

Alimony and Maintenance Payments

If you are divorced or separated, you may be receiving (or paying) amounts of alimony and/or maintenance. Generally, such payments are included in your income in the year of receipt (and are deductible for the payer in the same year). If the payment is taxable income to one party, it is an allowable deduction to the other. If the income is not taxable, the payment is not deductible.

Alimony or maintenance must be:

- periodic;
- pursuant to a decree, judgment, or written agreement; and
- made for the maintenance of the recipient and/or children.

In addition, the parties to the agreement must be living apart pursuant to a divorce, judicial separation, or written separation agreement, from the time of the payment until the end of the year. There are any number of complexities with respect to alimony and maintenance payments. These include whether the payments are periodic alimony or maintenance versus instalments of lump-sum obligations, and whether payments made to third parties qualify as alimony or maintenance, for example, payments made to the holder of the home mortgage. You should note that voluntary additional payments that are not part of the agreement will not qualify.

It is prudent to have competent legal and tax advice regarding separation and/or divorce agreements.

Frequently, alimony and maintenance agreements result in income shifting from a higher-income individual to a lower-income individual. As a result, there are tax benefits inherent in the payments because the higher-income individual obtains a deduction that saves a greater amount of tax than the corresponding tax cost to the recipient of the payment. Because of the shifting aspects of these payments, many separation or divorce agreements are negotiated on an after-tax basis.

Child Support Payments. As of May 1, 1997, child support paid pursuant to a written agreement or court order made on or after that day will neither be deductible by the payer, nor included in the income of the recipient for tax purposes. Existing child support orders will remain unaffected unless varied after April 30, 1997, to change the amount of the child support. After May 1, 1997, where the payer and the recipient of child support agree and file a joint election with Revenue Canada, they will be able to move to the new rules for payments after May 1, 1997, even if their agreement is not varied. Agreements entered into or court orders after March 5, 1996, can provide that the new rules will apply for payments made after May 1, 1997.

These tax changes do not apply to spousal support. Periodic payments of spousal support pursuant to a written agreement or order will be tax-deductible to the payer and taxable to the recipient. However, if an agreement or order does not clearly distinguish the amount of spousal support from child support, the entire amount will be deemed to be child support. Expenses paid to third parties will be treated as child support unless they are clearly identified in the agreement or order as being solely for the benefit of the recipient spouse. As well, child support will be deemed to have been paid before spousal support in cases of partial payment of the agreed amount.

Annuities

An annuity is an agreement for periodic payments over a specified period of time. It may be purchased with after-tax or before-tax dollars. For example, investing RRSP funds in an annuity contract uses before-tax dollars, while buying an annuity contract from savings uses after-tax dollars.

If an annuity payment is received from a contract purchased through a tax-exempt fund or plan, the full amount of the payment is includable in your taxable income in the year of receipt. Most common examples of such annuity payments include amounts from pension plans, RRSPs, and so forth.

If you have purchased the annuity with tax-paid funds rather than through a tax-exempt plan, a portion of each payment under the contract is excludable from your taxable income. This portion represents your original investment in the contract, which already has been taxed.

Gifts and Inheritances

The receipt of a gift or inheritance is not taxable income. The transferor is considered, with certain exceptions such as spousal transfers, to have sold the property at its fair market value at the date of transfer. Thus, the transferor will have taxable income on any accrued gains, while the recipient will be treated as having acquired the property at the fair market value at date of transfer.

Lotteries, Gambling, and Other Prize Winnings

Gains resulting from activities where the primary factor in determining whether there will be a gain is chance (e.g., lotteries and gambling) are not included in income. However, prizes related to your employment are likely to be considered as connected with services rendered, and thus taxable as employment income.

Other Deductions

Generally, personal expenditures are not deductible for tax purposes. However, you may deduct such miscellaneous items as fees for investment counselling, portfolio management fees, and safekeeping.

Child Care Expenses

This deduction is a maximum of $3,000 per child under age 16 at any time during the year. The maximum per child is increased to $5,000 for claims in respect of severely disabled children and children under seven years of age at the end of the year.

For federal tax purposes, the deduction is restricted to two-thirds of earned income and must be claimed by the lower-income spouse. However, for Quebec tax purposes, either spouse can claim the deduction, which is limited to the full earned income of the lower-income spouse.

CHAPTER THREE

Income Deferral

Income deferral simply means deferring the recognition of income for tax purposes to future years. The benefit of income deferral is that the payment of tax on that income is postponed. It is sometimes said that tax deferred is tax saved. If, for example, you can defer $1,000 of tax payable for one year, and earn 10 per cent during that time, you have "saved" $100 (less, of course, any tax payable on that $100 of income).

Over the past few years, there has been a significant drop in the number of opportunities to defer income, especially with respect to interest income, which must be reported annually even if it has not yet been received. These rules affect all taxpayers, including individuals and trusts with individuals as beneficiaries. However, income earned in deferred income plans, including registered retirement savings plans, deferred profit sharing plans, and registered pension plans, is not affected by these rules.

Three-Year Accrual Rules

The three-year accrual rules apply only to debt obligations acquired before 1990, but they apply to all debt obligations other than income bonds and debentures, Salary Deferral Arrangements (SDAs), Small Business Bonds (SBBs), and Small Business Development Bonds (SBDBs).

If an obligation held by an individual is subject to the three-year accrual rules, on every third anniversary date of the obligation, the individual must include in income any interest accrued and not previously included.

The "third anniversary" date is three years after December 31 of the calendar year in which the obligation was issued, and every third year thereafter. For purposes of determining the third anniversary date, obligations acquired before 1982 are deemed to have been issued on December 31, 1988; accordingly, the first third anniversary date was in 1991, the second in 1994, and so on.

You may elect in your tax return to include in income any interest accrued to the end of the year on a debt obligation that was not previously included in income. Once made, the election applies to that particular debt obligation for each subsequent year in which the taxpayer holds the obligation. Don't forget to think ahead. If you still hold investments that are subject to the three-year accrual rule and the operation of these rules will push your income into a higher tax bracket, you might be better off reporting the income annually. This is likely beneficial only if you would otherwise move from being taxed at the 17 per cent federal rate to the 26 per cent or 29 per cent federal rate. In making this election, however, remember that you must balance the tax saving against the fact that in future years you will also end up prepaying tax.

The interest accrual rules also apply where an individual holds an investment interest in a life insurance policy, including an annuity contract. The rules do not apply to "exempt policies", nor to most investment interests held before December 2, 1982. Certain prescribed annuity contracts are also exempt from the accrual rules.

If a taxpayer acquires a "prescribed debt obligation", interest is deemed to accrue on the obligation in a manner prescribed by regulation. Prescribed debt obligations include zero-interest bonds, bonds that are held without also holding the related bond interest coupons, and the interest coupons stripped from such bonds.

Annual Accrual Rules

The three-year accrual rules have been replaced by annual accrual rules for the investment instruments discussed above.

These rules apply to such investments acquired after 1989. You should be aware that an investment is treated as having been acquired after 1989 if, after that year, the term of the investment has been extended or the investment has been materially altered.

An obligation that is subject to the annual accrual rules requires, on each anniversary date of the instrument, an inclusion in income of any interest that has accrued and was not previously included in income. The first anniversary date is the day that is one year after the day immediately preceding the date on which the obligation was issued.

Issuers of investments subject to the annual accrual rules, including the Bank of Canada, are required to provide annual information slips to the holders of the instruments showing the amount of interest accrued to each anniversary date of the investment.

Planning Around the Accrual Rules. It goes without saying that before investing in deferred income securities or annuities, you should take maximum advantage of deferred income plans where you are not required to report income on an annual accrual basis. These include registered retirement savings plans (RRSPs) and registered pension plans (RPPs).

The earnings inside such plans are completely sheltered from tax until you withdraw funds from the plan. RRSP and RPP contributions are generally deductible from income in the current year, and payments from a plan can be postponed well into your retirement. Since the deferral is for the long term, you will generally benefit no matter what your marginal tax rate is when you eventually withdraw the funds.

For example, assume that you have the option of contributing $5,000 to an RRSP from which you will begin receiving a retirement income in 20 years. Your marginal tax rate now is 40 per cent, and in the table below it is assumed that your marginal rate in 20 years will be either 30 per cent or 40 per cent. To keep the example simple, it is assumed you will pay tax on the RRSP amount in a lump sum in the twentieth year, which of course would probably not be the case. The RRSP earns interest at the rate of 5 per cent over the 20 years.

Marginal Tax Rate	After-Tax Amount Available
30%	$9,287
40%	$7,960

If you did not make the RRSP contribution and paid tax at 40 per cent on the $5,000, you would have $3,000 left to invest. Assuming your annual after-tax return is 3 per cent (after paying tax at the rate of 40 per cent on 5 per cent earnings), you will accumulate $5,418 in 20 years, which is $2,542 less than you would accumulate by contributing to the RRSP (40 per cent tax rate after 20 years).

The advantage comes about because the before-tax amounts in the RRSP accumulate interest on a tax-free basis, while your after-tax earnings outside the plan are taxed each year and you have a smaller amount available for reinvestment. In addition, under the RRSP you are able to pay your taxes in the future with inflated dollars that are worth much less than today's dollars.

For a more comprehensive analysis of the retirement saving rules related to RRSPs, see Chapter 6.

You may also want to consider the possibility of deferring

tax by acquiring capital property. The accrual rules do not apply to unrealized capital gains. High-yield preferred shares may prove suitable, since they offer an attractive dividend with the possibility of capital gains. And the fact that the $500,000 lifetime capital gains exemption is still available for qualified farming property and shares of small business corporations makes owning such property even more attractive.

Retiring Allowances

To a certain extent, a retiring allowance can be considered as a means of deferring income. However, it must not take the form of a deferred salary, which would be the case if an employee accepted a relatively low salary in exchange for a generous so-called retiring allowance.

A retiring allowance is defined as an amount (other than a superannuation or pension benefit or an amount received as a consequence of the death of an employee) received by the employee on or after retirement in recognition of long service, including early retirement incentives or any payment received in respect of a loss of employment, whether or not received as a termination payment or damages from loss of office. Hence, termination payments are fully taxable, although the tax may be deferred by transferring eligible amounts to an RRSP.

Such a retiring allowance may be received by a dependant or relative of the taxpayer after his or her death or by his or her estate, and tax may also be deferred by transferring eligible amounts to his or her RRSP.

The maximum amount of a retiring allowance that can be transferred on a tax-free basis to a registered pension plan or RRSP is $3,500 for each calendar year before 1996 that the employee was employed by the employer paying the amount. If the employee was a member of the employer's pension plan or deferred profit sharing plan (DPSP), the maximum is reduced to $2,000 for each year the employer's contributions to such plans had vested in the employee. Only $2,000 a year for each year of service after 1988 and before 1996 may be transferred to an RRSP. Eligible amounts may still be transferred after 1995; however, the years after 1995 cannot be included in their calculation.

Any amount of a retiring allowance not transferred to either type of plan must be included in income in the year of receipt and will be taxed at your marginal rate.

If your retiring allowance is significant in relation to other sources of income, the alternative minimum tax may apply where the retiring allowance is transferred to an RRSP.

If the alternative minimum tax does apply, it may be recovered in one or more of the seven taxation years following the taxation year it is payable, depending on an individual's income and deductions in those years.

For Quebec tax purposes, beginning in 1997, the retiring allowance transferred to an RRSP will not be taken into consideration in calculating the Quebec alternative minimum tax.

Bear in mind that a retiring allowance cannot be transferred to a spousal RRSP.

You may want to arrange for your employer to transfer your retiring allowance directly to your RRSP, in which case no tax need be withheld.

If you receive the amount directly from your employer and then make the transfer, your employer must withhold tax, which you can then claim as a refund on your tax return.

Contributions to Deferred Profit Sharing Plans (DPSPs)

Your employer may be making deductible contributions to a DPSP on your behalf. The maximum employer contribution for 1996 is the lesser of 18 per cent of the employee's remuneration and $6,750, less any amount contributed by the employer on behalf of that employee to a registered pension plan. For the years

1997 to 2002, the total employer contribution will be limited to the lesser of 18 per cent of the employee's remuneration and $6,750, and will increase to $7,250 in 2003 and $7,750 in 2004.

The maximum figure will be indexed beginning in 2005 according to increases in the average wage. DPSPs must provide that the employer make a contribution based on company profits, but no contribution need be made in a loss year. A DPSP does not permit any type of past service contribution or employee contribution.

Proceeds from DPSPs. Amounts received from DPSPs must be included in income, except for capital amounts contributed by the employee for the years in which such contributions were permitted by law. Most plans allow for payment of taxable amounts to be spread over a maximum of ten years, or it is possible before reaching age 71 to purchase an annuity for life whose guaranteed terms, if any, cannot exceed 15 years. Employee contributions may be withdrawn at any time. DPSP proceeds also can be deferred by transferring them into a registered pension plan, an RRSP, or another eligible DPSP.

The above-mentioned age limit of 71 has been lowered to 69. However, this new limit will not apply to taxpayers reaching 70 at the end of 1996, nor will it apply to those who reach 69. The DPSPs of the latter will not have to be matured until the end of 1997.

Unpaid Remuneration

An employer is not allowed a deduction for remuneration expense in the year incurred if the amount remains unpaid to the employee more than 179 days after the year end of the employer.

Deferring remuneration therefore provides only a limited benefit. The employer will receive the deduction in the year the remuneration is actually paid. This provision applies whether or not the employer and employee are related. Remuneration expense does not include reasonable amounts for vacation or holiday pay, or deferred amounts under a salary deferral arrangement (SDA).

The salary deferral arrangement rules (see below) do not affect remuneration amounts paid within the 180-day limit. Thus, for the year the remuneration is earned, employees will not have to include a benefit in income for tax purposes equal to the unpaid amount.

Salary Deferral Arrangements. The rules concerning salary deferral arrangements were introduced to prevent abuses prevalent with respect to employee benefit plans.

A salary deferral arrangement is defined as a funded or unfunded plan involving an employee and employer under which the employee has postponed the receipt of his or her remuneration beyond the end of a year and it is reasonable to consider that one of the main purposes for the postponement is to defer the tax payable by the employee in respect of salary or wages for services rendered by him or her in the year or a preceding year. A variety of plans are excluded from the definition, including registered pension plans and other registered plans, certain benefit plans such as group sickness or accident insurance plans, plans to defer the salary of certain professional athletes, plans to provide funds for the education of workers, three-year bonus plans, and self-funded leave of absence plans.

In certain circumstances, the rules regarding salary deferral arrangements do not apply to plans in existence on February 26, 1986.

Under the salary deferral arrangement rules, a right to receive deferred amounts, whether funded or not, must be recognized for tax purposes on the accrual basis and be included in the employment income of the employee in the year the amount is earned, even if the amount is received at a later date. The employer will receive a deduction for the amount in that year. However, interest or other amounts paid by the employer in respect of the deferred salary will be treated as employment income in the year earned. For this reason, SDAs are excluded from the interest accrual rules. If a person besides the employee has a right to receive the deferred salary, these rules still come into play.

Retirement Compensation Arrangements. An RCA is generally any plan or arrangement established after October 8, 1986, under which payments are made by an employer or former employer (or related person) of a taxpayer to a custodian in connection with benefits to be provided to the taxpayer or others on the retirement, loss of office, etc., of the taxpayer. Certain arrangements are specifically excluded from the definition, such as registered pension plans, employee profit sharing plans and DPSPs, RRSPs, group sickness and accident insurance plans, certain plans established for professional athletes and officials, and SDAs.

Contributions to an RCA are deductible by the employer when made but are subject to a refundable 50 per cent withholding tax (except for Quebec tax purposes). This tax is refunded when payments are made from the RCA and included in the recipient's income. Income earned in the RCA on the contributions is also subject to a 50 per cent tax that is refundable when payments are made to beneficiaries. Any income from an RCA is not taxable to the recipient until actually received.

Employee Benefit Plans. In the unlikely event that a deferral plan does not fall within the definition of a salary deferral arrangement or a retirement compensation arrangement, it is likely that the plan is an employee benefit plan (EBP), in which case the employer will not receive a deduction for amounts deferred. (Prior to the introduction of the SDA rules, employee benefit plans were frequently used to defer the salary of employees who worked for non-taxable employers, such as government, non-profit organizations, or companies in a loss position.)

Under such a plan, a portion of the employee's salary is placed with a custodian. The employer receives no deduction for amounts directed to the custodian, and the employee is not taxed on such amounts until they are actually received. Investment income earned on the deferred amounts is taxed in the hands of the plan, or in the hands of the employee or employer. This is the case for self-funded leave of absence arrangements, under which an employee may defer up to one-third of his or her salary each year for up to six years. The deferred amount must be included in the income of the employee for tax purposes in the seventh year.

Shareholder Loans

If a shareholder or a person related to the shareholder receives a loan or incurs any type of indebtedness (other than loans described below) from the shareholder's corporation or a related corporation, and the amount is not repaid by the end of the lender's following taxation year, the amount of the loan is included in the debtor's income in the year the loan was made. This may necessitate amending that year's income tax return. If the amount is included in income and is repaid at a later date, it is deductible from income in the year of repayment. However, a series of loans and repayments would not qualify for this treatment. Furthermore, in the year of repayment, you should ensure that you have sufficient income to absorb any deduction due to repayment of such a loan.

There are four other exceptions to the rules requiring a loan to be included in income:

- when the creditor lends the money as part of its ordinary business;
- when loans are made to employees of the creditor or their spouses to enable or assist them to purchase a dwelling for their own habitation;

- when loans are made to employees of the creditor to enable or assist them to purchase an automobile to be used by them while performing the duties of their employment;
- when a corporate creditor lends funds to employees to enable or assist them to purchase, from the corporation or a related corporation, fully paid treasury shares of the corporation to be held by them for their own benefit.

This last provision does not provide for the employee to purchase shares from any other shareholder; rather, they must be purchased directly from the corporation.

In each of the four cases, bona fide arrangements must be in place at the time the loan is made for repayment of the loan or indebtedness within a reasonable period.

The taxable benefit rules regarding imputed interest on low-interest or interest-free employee loans apply, for the most part, to all types of shareholder loans and indebtedness (see Chapter 2). However, home purchase and home relocation loan rules don't apply to shareholder loans unless the shareholder is an employee and the loan was received because of the borrower's status as an employee. Advances to shareholders during the year in anticipation of dividend payments are considered to be indebtedness, and the imputed interest taxable benefit rules apply.

The act under which a corporation is incorporated may contain rules about lending money to employees, officers, directors, and shareholders of the corporation; therefore, reference should be made to this act before any such loan is made.

CHAPTER FOUR

Income Splitting

Income splitting occurs when income that normally would be taxed entirely in your hands is taxed in the hands of both you and another person with a lower marginal tax rate, for example, your spouse (including a common-law spouse) or children. If the difference in marginal tax rates is 20 per cent, the family's tax saving is $200 for every $1,000 of income transferred to the lower-rate individual (assuming the transfer does not bump the transferee into a higher tax bracket).

However, the government is aware of this benefit, and the Income Tax Act contains provisions, called the attribution rules, that are designed to discourage income splitting. These rules have the effect of attributing the income back to you, so that it is taxed in your hands, despite the fact that you have not personally received it.

The first part of this chapter points out where income splitting may still be used to achieve tax savings (situations where the attribution rules do not apply). The second part presents situations where the attribution rules apply and, consequently, where income splitting does not produce any decrease in taxes.

Getting Around the Attribution Rules

Generally, it has become difficult, if not impossible, to have large amounts of income taxed in your spouse's or children's hands rather than in your hands over a short period of time. It is now important to begin your income splitting program as early as possible and continually update it. The various planning options discussed below assume that you have and will continue to have a higher tax rate than your spouse and children.

Business Income

The attribution rules do not generally apply to business income earned by your spouse or child with transferred or lent funds. Thus, if you give your spouse or child money to finance a personally run business, or invest in a partnership in which your spouse or child actively participates, income from that business should not be attributed to you; however, any capital gain that arises on disposition of the business by your spouse would be attributed to you. There is no attribution of capital gains earned by your minor child except where the property is farm property that previously received preferential tax treatment. The attribution rules also should not apply if you and your spouse operate a business as a bona fide partnership.

If you have lent or transferred to a person property that is an interest in a partnership, that person's share of the business income of the partnership may be considered income from property (and not income from business) for purposes of the attribution rules, and may therefore be attributed back to you.

This provision will apply where the person is a "specified member" of the partnership. This occurs where the person

- was a limited partner of the partnership during the fiscal period in which the income arose; and
- was neither actively engaged in the activities of the partnership nor carried on a business similar to that of the partnership (other than as a member of the partnership) on a regular, continuous, and substantial basis throughout the period.

For example, you give or lend your spouse $100,000 that is used to acquire an interest in a limited partnership. Under the attribution rules, if your spouse is only a passive investor and if your spouse's share of the partnership income is $10,000 for a given year, that $10,000 will be added to your income for the year, not to that of your spouse.

Interest on Interest

The attribution rules do not mean that you should abandon the idea of giving or lending your spouse or children funds to earn investment income. The fact that interest on interest is not attributed can be significant in the long run. For example, if you give your spouse $20,000, which is invested to earn 8 per cent annually over the next ten years with the interest paid annually and reinvested at this same rate, then only the simple interest of $16,000 (8 per cent of $20,000 = $1,600 × 10 years) will be attributed to you. Interest on interest of $7,178, over and above the simple interest of $16,000, will be earned over the ten-year period, if the annual interest of $1,600 is reinvested at 8 per cent, and it will be taxed in your spouse's hands, not in yours.

Generally speaking, there is no attribution of income earned on attributed income, such as interest on interest, except where the attributed income is a stock dividend. Moreover, although the income or gain is attributed for tax purposes, these amounts still legally belong to the spouse or minor.

Spousal Registered Retirement Savings Plans

Because of the attribution rules, taxpayers should definitely consider making use of spousal RRSPs.

Details on spousal RRSPs are contained in Chapter 6.

The principal advantage of contributing to a spousal RRSP is the achievement of future income splitting, since the attribution rules do not apply. The annuity or registered retirement income fund (RRIF) payments eventually arising from the spousal RRSP are taxable in the hands of your spouse, and not in your hands.

If there is some chance that you will need to withdraw RRSP funds in the near future, you should ensure that any spousal RRSP contributions are made to a separate plan. Any funds withdrawn from your spouse's RRSP can be attributed to you if you contributed to this RRSP during the year or during the two years preceding the withdrawal. Remember that amounts contributed to a spousal RRSP belong to your spouse.

If you contribute to your spouse's RRSP, you should make the payment directly to the trustee and have it receipted to you, so that you can prove you made the payment.

Paying Your Spouse's Taxes

If your income is higher than your spouse's, you might consider paying your spouse's taxes as another method of effectively transferring funds to your spouse.

This amount would be considered a gift by you to your spouse. Of course, no income would be earned on the amount since it is used to pay taxes, and therefore there would be no attribution. Your spouse could then invest the funds that otherwise would have gone to pay his or her taxes, and any income earned on these funds would not be attributed back to you. This arrangement would not work if your spouse's taxes were deducted at source by an employer.

Paying Family Expenses

If both spouses are earning income but one spouse will continually have a higher tax rate than the other, the higher-income spouse should consider paying all or most of the family expenses, and the lower-income spouse invest all or most of his or her earnings.

The income generated from these investments will be taxed at a lower rate.

Transferring the Child Tax Benefit

The most common method of generating income that is taxable in the hands of a child is to place federal Child Tax Benefit cheques for that child in the child's own investment vehicle, such as a savings account, bonds, or investment certificates. The income earned on these funds will not be attributed back to you.

Maintaining a Dependant's Status

If the child has qualifying "earned income", a contribution could be made to an RRSP on behalf of the child. This will lower the child's income and, together with tuition fees and other deductions/credits, may place the child in a dependent category, allowing the parent to claim the child as a dependant and/or to use a portion of the child's tuition fee and education tax credits.

Paying Your Spouse or Child a Salary

You may pay your spouse or child a salary for work performed in your unincorporated business, and deduct the salary in determining your income from the business. The amount will be taxed in your spouse's or child's hands. The salary or wages paid must be reasonable in relation to the duties performed. Your spouse or child may then be in a position to contribute to the Canada Pension Plan and also to an RRSP.

Spousal Business Partnerships

Even though you may pay a salary to your spouse, there may be reasons why you want to establish that the business is actually a partnership, thereby entitling the spouse to a share of partnership profits. This situation is common in farm operations, but may apply to any type of business.

You should establish a properly documented partnership agreement detailing the profit-sharing arrangements and ownership of assets of the business.

If Revenue Canada considers the allocation of the partnership income to be unreasonable, it will change it to an allocation that it considers reasonable in the circumstances.

If the spouse's capital contribution to the business is significant, a spousal partnership generally will be more advantageous than paying the spouse a salary. This could permit a larger share of the business profits to be recognized by the spouse than if the spouse were paid a reasonable salary for duties performed.

If, for example, you are operating a sideline business that has a reasonable expectation of medium-term profit, it may be advantageous to pay your spouse a reasonable salary, thereby creating a loss in the business for a given year. This may be the case if you have other sources of income against which the losses can be applied.

If you cannot establish a spousal partnership, you could consider incorporating the business and your spouse could participate by owning shares acquired with his or her own funds.

Transfers at Fair Market Value

You may elect to transfer property to your spouse and receive fair market value consideration for it. Under certain conditions, the attribution rules will not apply, and future income and capital gains will be taxed in your spouse's hands. For capital property, this means that you would have to recognize any accrued capital gains or losses at the time of the transfer.

If property with unrealized capital losses is transferred at fair market value, the superficial loss rules come into play, and you will be denied the capital loss if the property is still owned by your spouse 31 days after the transfer.

Gift Interest Expense to Your Spouse

Income must be earned or a capital gain realized on funds transferred or gifted to your spouse for the attribution rules to be applied. Hence, there is no attribution if no income is earned on the transferred funds. Similarly, if you give your spouse funds to pay the interest on a loan made by you to your spouse, there should be no attribution in respect of the amount gifted for the interest expense, nor attribution of the net income earned by the spouse from the lent funds. Of course, the loan must be a bona fide loan, interest must be charged at the lesser of the prescribed rate for tax purposes and commercial rates, and the interest must be paid within 30 days of the year end.

You must include the interest paid by the spouse in income for tax purposes, but you will benefit because the spouse's investment income will compound much more quickly since it is not being diluted annually by an interest payment on the loan.

Using Transferred Funds for Leverage

The income or capital gains earned on funds borrowed by your spouse on a commercial basis with no guarantee by you is not attributable. Thus, if you were considering borrowing for investment purposes, you might consider transferring funds to your spouse that would enable him or her to borrow. For example, you might give your spouse $25,000 and he or she would then borrow $75,000. The spouse then buys $100,000 worth of securities, which would be lodged as collateral with the lending institution in lieu of your guarantee. In this situation, only 25 per cent of any net income or capital gains earned ($25,000/$100,000) would be attributed to you.

Locking in the Best Rate on Spousal Loans

If you intend to lend funds to your spouse, you will generally charge interest at the prescribed rate (the rate applicable to late tax payments and overpayments of tax), which usually will be lower than commercial lending rates. The prescribed rate is set each quarter based on 90-day Treasury Bill yields of the first month of the preceding quarter. Thus, the rate for any quarter is known about two months in advance. Before locking in the interest rate on a spousal loan for any longer than three months, you should determine the direction the prescribed rate will move in the next quarter. If the rate is expected to increase, and you do not expect rates to fall again, you might consider setting the term of the loan for an extended period. If the rate is expected to decline, you should keep the loan on a variable-rate basis.

Professional Management Companies

Professional management companies are popular because the attribution rules do not apply to small business corporations. Such companies are generally set up by professionals such as doctors or dentists who are not allowed by their governing bodies to incorporate. The company, which is owned by the spouse and/or children of the professional, provides services to the professional and is paid a fee, usually about 15 per cent above the cost of the services. Such services could include the rental of equipment and facilities; the services of assistants; and bookkeeping, secretarial, and administrative services. When arranging such a corporation, professional advice should be sought to ensure the company will not be considered a personal services business, which has certain limitations on expenses and affects the rate of tax the corporation will pay.

If it is incorporated, such a business is considered a small business corporation and no attribution of income will occur if the professional lends or sells assets to a small business corporation in which a spouse or children are shareholders. If the management business is unincorporated, which is generally not advisable, and assets are transferred to the spouse and used to earn business income, there would be no attribution of that income.

Depending on the nature of services provided, fees billed for these services may be subject to the GST and, in Quebec, the Quebec Sales Tax.

Some activities, such as most health care services, do not qualify for a reimbursement of the GST and QST paid. In such cases, the use of a professional management company may be disadvantageous.

A Word of Caution

Some of the above suggestions are "aggressive", i.e., the tax authorities may not take kindly to taxpayers using them. If you are considering any of these aggressive techniques, you should consult your professional advisors to identify any possible disadvantages. In many cases, you will not be worse off if the plan is scuttled somehow or other, since the attributed income or capital gain would have been realized in your hands in any case.

Situations Where the Attribution Rules Apply

The following are situations where the attribution rules apply and, consequently, where the tax savings are nearly impossible to achieve.

Transfers to Your Spouse or Minor Children

The attribution rules apply if an individual lends or transfers property to, or for the benefit of, a spouse (or future spouse) or certain minors, or a trust established for such a person. The attribution rules apply to minors (under age 18) with whom the individual does not deal at arm's length (child, grandchild, brother, sister, brother-in-law, sister-in-law, etc.) and to an individual's niece or nephew. As well, rules similar to the attribution rules apply where property is lent to any non-arm's-length person, such as an adult child. Property includes money, shares, bonds, a right of any kind, a home, or land. The word "transfer" has been interpreted very broadly. For example, it includes a gift, or may include a sale at fair market value.

If the attribution rules apply, income (or losses) from lent or transferred property, or from property substituted for it, is not taxed in the hands of the recipient spouse, but is included in the income of the individual who made the loan or transfer. In most cases, it is the net income or loss from the property that is attributed to the lender or transferor.

The attribution rules also apply to capital gains and losses realized by a spouse on lent or transferred property or substituted property. There is no attribution of capital gains or losses realized by a minor (under age 18 throughout the taxation year), except in certain cases involving farm property that has been previously given preferential tax treatment.

Capital gains are attributable to the transferor only for transfers occurring after 1971. Thus, a capital gain arising from property transferred before 1972 is not attributable, but any income earned on that property, such as dividends, is attributable to the transferor.

Attribution Rules and Trusts

For there to be attribution of income (or loss), the spouse or minor child must initially have an income (except in certain corporate situations). For example, if property is transferred to a trust for the benefit of minor children and the income from the property is taxed in the trust, there is no attribution of income. (Note, however, that all of the income of an *inter vivos* trust is taxed at the highest personal tax rate and no advantage would be gained.) If the income is paid or payable to the children from the trust, it therefore constitutes income and the attribution rules will apply. However, a net loss suffered by a trust cannot be allocated to beneficiaries and, consequently, there can never be attribution of trust losses.

If the attributed income is earned through a trust, special rules apply to determine how much trust income of a designated beneficiary (i.e., the spouse, minor child, minor niece or nephew) is attributed. These rules will produce different results depending on whether all or only a portion of the income earned by the trust is from "lent or transferred property", or whether there is more than one designated beneficiary.

If you and your spouse each decide to contribute funds to the same trust, which includes your minor child as a beneficiary, the income of that minor would seem to be attributed to both you and your spouse, which would lead to double taxation. However, if each parent created a separate trust, only the income of one trust would be attributed back to the parent who created it.

If you are involved in trusts, you should review your situation to ensure you do not inadvertently stumble into unfortunate tax complications.

The attributed income retains its character (except in corporate attribution situations). For example, if an individual lends funds to his or her spouse who invests the funds in preferred shares, any dividends or capital gains, or capital losses on the preferred shares, will be attributed back to the individual who will treat the amounts as dividends, capital gains, or capital losses.

Substituted Property. The attribution rules apply not only to lent or transferred property but also to property that is substituted for the lent or transferred property. For example, if an individual lends funds to his or her spouse, who uses the funds to acquire preferred shares, the shares are substituted property and the attribution rules would apply to the income from, and capital gains or losses on, the shares. If the preferred shares were sold and the funds were used to acquire bonds, the bonds would be substituted property to which the attribution rules would apply.

The definition of substituted property states that a stock dividend received on a share will be considered property substituted for that share. Accordingly, the attribution rules will apply to any income earned (and in the case of a spouse, any gains realized) on a stock dividend that was received as income on lent, transferred, or substituted property.

No Attribution. In the case of a related minor, attribution of income generally ceases the year the child turns 18 (see "Property Lent to Non-Arm's-Length Party" below). In the case of a spouse, attribution ceases upon divorce or when the spouses are living separate and apart by reason of marriage breakdown. The transferor/lender spouse must file an election (which is a joint election with the transferee/borrower) for the attribution of capital gains not to occur after the breakdown of a marriage. Attribution also stops when a lender or transferor dies or ceases to be resident in Canada.

In addition, income from certain loans or transfers is not subject to attribution.

The attribution rules may not apply to a loan if

- interest is charged on the loan at a reasonable rate or at the rate prescribed for income tax purposes at the time the loan was made; and
- the interest payable for each year is paid within 30 days after the end of that year.

In the case of a transfer, there is no attribution if

- the fair market value (FMV) of the transferred property does not exceed the FMV of the consideration received by the transferor on the transfer;
- where the consideration received includes debt, the conditions listed above for an exempt loan are met; and
- where the property is transferred to a spouse, the transferor elects not to have the tax-deferred rollover provisions apply.

Property Lent to Non-Arm's-Length Party

Income attribution applies when an individual lends property to another individual with whom he or she does not deal at arm's length, and it is reasonable to consider that one of the main reasons for the loan is to reduce or avoid tax on income from the property (or property substituted for it) by causing such income to be included in the income of the other individual.

This application of attribution rules covers loans between individuals who are connected by blood relationship (forebears and descendants), marriage, or adoption. Parents, spouses, and even adult children are affected. The outright transfer of property to a non-arm's-length individual is, however, not affected.

The typical situation covered by this rule is a low-interest or no-interest loan made to your adult child. There is an exemption from the new rule if you charge a commercial rate of interest. If, however, the rate of interest is less than both the prescribed interest rate for income tax purposes (announced quarterly) and the rate that arm's-length parties would have agreed to under similar circumstances when the loan was made, income attribution will still apply. It will also apply if the interest on the loan is not paid within 30 days after the end of each year. If the debtor spends the funds for a non-investment purpose (e.g., paying tuition fees), there is no income to attribute.

Corporate Attribution Rules

These rules apply to loans and transfers made after October 27, 1986. In very broad terms, they operate as follows: when one of the main purposes of the loan or transfer may reasonably be considered to be to reduce the individual's income and to benefit a "designated person", unless the individual receives (as a minimum) an annual prescribed return on the debt or shares received on the loan or transfer of property, there will be deemed attribution of interest income to the individual. A designated person means a spouse or certain minors if they own at least 10 per cent of any class of shares of the corporation.

The corporate attribution rules do not apply to small business corporations (SBCs). The SBC must be a Canadian-controlled private corporation (CCPC) that primarily carries on an active business in Canada. A public corporation cannot be an SBC, nor can CCPCs that hold portfolio investments or real estate.

The rules are very broad. The following comments highlight some potential problems.

- The attribution rules can apply where the shareholders of the corporation to which an individual has lent or transferred property include the individual's spouse, certain minors, or a partnership or trust in which the spouse or a minor is, respectively, a member or a beneficiary.

- Unlike the normal attribution rules discussed above, the spouse or a minor need not receive income for the corporate attribution rules to apply.

Corporate attribution rules do not apply when the shares of the corporation are held in trust, and under the terms of the trust the individual may not receive any of the capital or income of the trust while he or she is a designated person (spouse, related minor, niece, or nephew).

Testamentary Planning

If your children are grown and have their own minor children, you might consider bequeathing funds in your will in trust to your grandchildren rather than your adult children. On your death, the funds would go in trust, with your children as trustees, to the minor grandchildren. There would be no attribution, since the attribution rules cease to apply on the death of the transferor. The grandchildren would earn income on the bequeathed funds and be taxed at a much lower rate than if their parents (your children) had earned the income. The parents could direct the trust to use the funds and income for the education costs of your grandchildren.

Farm Property Transfers to a Child

There is an exception where capital gains do not have to be recognized by the transferor on certain transfers to a child. A transfer during your lifetime of farm property to a child, grandchild, or great-grandchild may be made at any value between your adjusted cost base of the farming property and its fair market value. The child assumes a tax cost equal to the transfer value and becomes liable for any capital gains on disposition. However, if the child disposes of the farming property, including farming assets, before the year he or she turns 18, any capital gain will be attributed to you.

A farm property is one of which substantially all the assets are used in farming. The property must be actively farmed by the transferor or any family member immediately before transfer, and the child must be a Canadian resident. Such a tax-deferred transfer is also allowed for an interest in a qualifying farm partnership and for shares of farm corporations.

A full $500,000 capital gains exemption is available on the disposition of qualified farm property. If you have already claimed the full exemption under the $100,000 lifetime exemption that was available on other property until 1994, the exemption in respect of qualified farm property is $400,000.

Unless you otherwise expect to fully use your exemption, your children will be better off (i.e., will have a smaller gain to realize in the future) if you transfer the farm property at a value above your cost and recognize all or a portion of any resulting gain that would be exempt under your $500,000 lifetime capital gains exemption.

CHAPTER FIVE

Personal Tax Credits

The Essentials

Unlike tax deductions, tax credits provide the same dollar benefit to each taxpayer claiming a particular credit because the credit is subtracted directly from the individual's tax payable. If, however, the individual has no tax payable from which the credit can be deducted, and the credit is not refundable, the value of the credit is lost.

It makes sense to be aware of the personal tax credits that exist, so that you can take advantage of them whenever possible. You should also be sensitive to some of the differences between the various credits. Note that the dollar values used in this chapter represent the federal credits, which are deducted before computing provincial tax. (The Quebec system differs from that in the other provinces. See Chapter 13.) The total credits are therefore worth more than the federal-only dollar values used in this chapter.

Single Status

The federal single status tax credit for individuals for 1996 is $1,098. The federal credit is indexed annually according to increases in the Consumer Price Index above 3 per cent.

Spouse Credit

In 1996, a person who at any time in the year is a married person supporting a spouse with net income of $538 or less may claim a federal married tax credit of $915. The credit is reduced by 17 per cent of the spouse's net income in excess of $538. Thus, no credit is available for a spouse whose net income is $5,918 or more. If you live apart from your spouse at the end of the year by reason of marriage breakdown, any reduction in the spouse credit is calculated using your spouse's income for the year while married and not separated. The credit may also be claimed by a taxpayer who supports his or her common-law spouse.

You may claim the credit for only one person. If you divorce and remarry in the same year, you won't double the credit. The federal spouse tax credit is indexed annually according to increases in the Consumer Price Index above 3 per cent.

Equivalent-to-Spouse

The equivalent-to-spouse tax credit may be claimed by individuals who support a wholly dependent person and are unmarried, or married but did not support or live with the spouse. The federal credit is $915 in 1996, reduced by 17 per cent of the dependant's income over $538. If the dependant's income is $5,918 or more, the credit is nil.

To claim the credit, you must, whether alone or in concert with others, maintain a self-contained domestic establishment in which you live and support the dependant. The dependant must be related to you, wholly dependent on you (or on you and certain others) for support, and must be resident in Canada, unless the dependant is your child. Except in the case of a parent or grandparent, the dependant must be either under 18 years of age at any time in the year or dependent by reason of mental or physical infirmity.

An individual may claim the equivalent-to-spouse credit in respect of only one other person, and no more than one individual may claim the credit for the same person or the same self-contained domestic establishment. If two or more individuals could otherwise claim the credit for the same dependant or the same self-contained domestic establishment, they must agree which one will claim the credit. In the absence of agreement, the credit will apparently not be allowed to any of them.

If you are entitled to claim the equivalent-to-spouse credit in respect of a person, neither you nor anyone else may claim a dependant tax credit in respect of that person. The equivalent-to-spouse federal tax credit is indexed annually according to increases in the Consumer Price Index above 3 per cent.

Dependants

"Dependant" means a child or grandchild of you or your spouse or, if resident in Canada at any time in the year, a parent, grandparent, brother, sister, uncle, aunt, niece, or nephew of you or your spouse.

If a person is dependent on you by reason of mental or physical infirmity and is not under 18 years of age at any time in the year, you may claim a dependant tax credit of $400 in 1996, provided the dependant's income does not exceed $4,103. The credit is eroded if the dependant's income exceeds $4,103, and is reduced to nil if the dependant's income is $6,456 or more. The credit is indexed annually according to increases in the Consumer Price Index above 3 per cent.

If a dependant is claimed under the equivalent-to-spouse tax credit described above, that person cannot also be claimed as a dependant with a mental or physical infirmity.

If more than one individual is entitled to claim a dependant tax credit in respect of the same dependant, the total claimed by such individuals must not exceed the maximum allowed if only one individual were to make the claim. The tax department may allocate the total tax credit to the supporting individuals if they cannot agree on an allocation.

Age 65 and Over

A taxpayer who attained the age of 65 years before the end of 1996 may be able to claim a $592 federal tax credit. This credit is 17 per cent of the "age amount" ($3,482 currently). The age amount is reduced by 15 per cent of the individual's net income exceeding $25,921. If you are unable to make full use of the credit, all or a portion of it can be transferred to your spouse. The federal credit is indexed annually according to increases in the Consumer Price Index above 3 per cent.

Mental or Physical Impairment

Persons with a severe and prolonged mental or physical impairment that has been certified by a medical doctor or optometrist may claim a federal tax credit in 1996 of $720. This federal credit is indexed annually according to increases in the Consumer Price Index above 3 per cent. Any unused portion of the credit may, under certain circumstances, be transferred to a spouse or to another person who supported the individual.

Pension Income

If you attained age 65 before the end of 1996, you may claim a maximum federal tax credit of $170 in respect of your pension income, provided that income is at least $1,000. If it is less than $1,000, the maximum credit is 17 per cent of the pension income. A similar credit is available in respect of "qualified pension income" for taxpayers who are under 65 at the end of the year.

If you cannot make full use of your pension income tax credit, the unused portion may be transferred to your spouse. The pension tax credit is not subject to indexation and therefore remains at the level at which it was introduced in 1988.

CPP/QPP and Employment Insurance Credit

The federal CPP/QPP and EI tax credit is calculated as 17 per cent of CPP/QPP and EI payments for the year. Both the employee contribution and the "employer" amount that self-employed persons contribute to the CPP/QPP have been converted from a deduction to a credit.

For 1996, the maximum EI payments are $1,610.70 for

employers and $1,150.50 for employees, while the maximum CPP payment is $893.20 by both employers and employees.

Charitable Donations

The federal tax credit on qualifying charitable donations is 17 per cent on the first $200 donated and 29 per cent on donations above $200. Thus, the total credit on a $1,000 donation for an individual in the top tax bracket (assuming a 55 per cent rate of provincial tax) in 1996 will be about $434:

Federal credit at 17% on first $200 donated	$ 34.00
Federal credit at 29% on excess ($800)	232.00
Total federal credits	266.00
Surtax reduction	21.28
	287.28
Provincial tax reduction at 55% of $266	146.30
Total tax reduction	$433.58

The annual limit on qualifying donations to charitable institutions is 50 per cent of net income. As well, any donation not claimed under the tax credit system still may be carried forward for five years. However, in the carry-forward year, the 17 per cent rate applies to the first $200 of all donations against which a credit is claimed, including carry-forward donations. This may result in a small tax cost if you were not otherwise donating $200 in that year.

Where appreciated capital property is gifted, the 50 per cent limit is further increased by one-half of the taxable gain arising from the gifted property. In this case, the donation limit would equal 100 per cent of the net income that arises as a consequence of the gift. Also, in the year of death and in the immediately preceding taxation year, the limit on gifts, including bequests or legacies, is 100 per cent of the individual's net income.

Claiming credit for $400 on one spouse's return (rather than each spouse claiming $200) saves tax because half the donation qualifies for the 29 per cent federal rate rather than the 17 per cent rate.

Medical Expenses

The federal tax credit for 1996 in respect of medical expenses is 17 per cent of an amount that is calculated by subtracting from your total qualifying medical expenses the lesser of $1,614 and 3 per cent of your net income for the year. (The $1,614 amount is indexed annually according to increases in the Consumer Price Index above 3 per cent.) Receipts for the medical expenses must be filed when claiming the tax credit, and the expenses must not have been used previously. If the claimant dies within the year, the medical expenses must be paid within any 24-month period including the date of death. In any other case, they must be paid within any 12-month period ending in the taxation year. You should choose this 12-month period carefully, as it can affect the size of your tax credit. The Income Tax Act contains extensive provisions detailing the nature of expenditures that qualify as medical expenses.

Tuition Fees

The 1996 federal tuition fee tax credit is 17 per cent of eligible tuition fees paid in the year to a qualified institution for courses at the post–secondary school level, or to an institution certified by the Minister of Employment and Immigration (for courses intended to provide occupational skills to a student who is at least age 16 at the end of the year), provided the total of such fees paid in the year to that institution exceeds $100. Special rules also extend the tax credit to eligible tuition fees paid by a full-time student enrolled at a university outside Canada, and to fees greater than $100 paid by a Canadian resident who commutes to an educational institution providing courses at the post-secondary level in the United States.

Only tuition fees paid in respect of the year are eligible to determine the tuition tax credit for that year. Where the tuition fees paid in a particular year cover the tuition required for an academic session extending beyond that particular year, they are eligible in determining the tuition tax credit for the year to which they relate. For example, where the session covered by the tuition fees extends from September of one year to April of the next year, the tuition tax credit is computed for each of those years as one-half of the total tuition fees paid multiplied by 17 per cent.

Any unused portion (up to $850) of the tuition fee tax credit and the education tax credit (see below) may be transferred for use by the student's spouse. If the spouse did not claim the student as a dependant and did not claim any of the student's unused tax credits that could have been transferred to the spouse, the student's supporting parent or grandparent may claim the student's unused tuition fee and education tax credits (to a maximum of $850). A prescribed form must be filed by the parent or grandparent making the claim.

Education

The federal education tax credit for 1996 is $17 for each month in the year during which you were a full-time student in a qualifying program at a designated educational institution. To claim the tax credit, you must file a certificate issued by the educational institution. (Full-time enrolment is not required if you qualify for the disability tax credit, or your doctor or optometrist certifies that your impairment makes full-time enrolment unreasonable.)

Child Tax Benefit

The former family allowance payments, the refundable child tax credit, and the non-refundable tax credit for dependent children were replaced in 1993 by the child tax benefit that is paid monthly, usually to the mother.

The annual benefit of $1,020 per child increases by $75 for the third and each subsequent child in a family, and by $213 per child under age seven if no child care expenses have been claimed. For low-income families, the child tax benefit also includes a Working Income Supplement of up to $500 per family (increasing to $750 July 1, 1997, and $1,000 July 1, 1998). The benefit is reduced for higher-income families. It is not subject to income tax, and it is indexed annually according to changes in the Consumer Price Index above 3 per cent.

Political Contributions

A federal tax credit is available for contributions to a registered political party or an officially nominated candidate in a federal election. The credit is based on the amount contributed and is calculated on a sliding scale, $500 being the maximum credit for any one taxation year.

Amount Contributed	Tax Credit Available
$1–$100	75% of the contribution
$100–$550	$75 plus 50% of excess over $100
$550–$1,150	$300 plus one-third of excess over $550
Over $1,150	$500

All provinces and territories except Saskatchewan also permit tax credits for political contributions, but the credit is deducted from provincial tax payable, and contributions must be made to provincial political parties or associations, or to candidates standing for provincial election.

The tax credit in British Columbia, Manitoba, Newfoundland, Nova Scotia, New Brunswick, Prince Edward Island, and the Yukon Territory is calculated in the same manner as for federal purposes, the maximum credit being $500. In the Northwest Territories, the credit is 100 per cent of the first $100 contributed and 50 per cent of the excess over $100, to a maximum credit of $500. The maximum credit in Ontario is $750, calculated as 75 per cent of the first $200, 50 per cent of the next $600, and 33-1/3 per cent of the next $900. The maximum credit in Alberta is also $750, calculated as 75 per cent of the first $150 contributed, 50 per cent of the next $675, and 33-1/3 per cent of the next $900. In Quebec, the tax credit is calculated as 75 per cent of the first $200 contributed and 50 per cent of the next $200, the maximum credit being $250.

Official receipts must be filed with your tax return to receive the credit. Generally, political contributions must be made in the form of cash or other negotiable instruments (cheques, money orders, etc.). However, some provinces permit the contribution of goods or services under certain conditions.

Political contributions in excess of $1,150 ($900 in the Northwest Territories, $400 in Quebec, $1,725 in Alberta, and $1,700 in Ontario) in any one taxation year will be lost for purposes of receiving the tax credit. If the tax credit exceeds your federal or provincial tax payable after the deduction of other credits, you are not allowed to claim a refund of tax or carry forward any excess credit to a future taxation year.

Planning for Your Contributions. If you are making a large contribution, you should attempt to spread it over two years. This strategy is recommended in any case since you will be able to take advantage of the larger credits available. For example, if you contribute $1,000 in one year, your credit is $450 (except in the Northwest Territories, Quebec, Ontario, and Alberta). If you contribute $500 this year and $500 next year, your total credit is $550, giving you a $100 tax saving. This same technique should also be applied if both spouses earn taxable income, except the spouses would split their contribution in the year (i.e., each spouse would contribute $500, instead of one spouse contributing $1,000). Splitting the contribution is beneficial because the maximum percentage credit applies at lower contribution levels.

CHAPTER SIX

Saving for Retirement

An RRSP is an investment vehicle in which you invest pre-tax employment or self-employed income within specific limits. No tax is paid on income earned in the RRSP. Eventually, you arrange for the accumulated amount in your plan to be paid back to you as retirement income, at which time the payments are subject to tax. RRSPs may also be used effectively for saving for a down payment on a home or a year's sabbatical from your job. Withdrawing RRSP funds for these purposes, however, should be done only as a last resort, since it destroys the main RRSP function of generating an adequate retirement income.

MAKING AN RRSP WORK FOR YOU

Because your RRSP contribution allows you claim a deduction on your income tax return, you retain the tax that you otherwise would have to pay on the amount of the contribution. That gives you more money to invest within the RRSP than you would have if you paid the tax and used after-tax dollars to invest outside an RRSP. If you pay the tax now, those dollars are gone forever. If you contribute to an RRSP, you get to use those tax dollars as part of your investment program and, depending on your age, you may get to do so for a very long time. That's how saving tax dollars now can give you a powerful boost toward a financially worry-free retirement.

The longer the funds remain in your RRSP, the better off you will be investing in your RRSP than investing outside it. That's why you should begin making RRSP contributions as early in your working life as possible. The earlier you begin contributing to an RRSP, the more you maximize your contribution each year, and the earlier you contribute each year, the more will be available in the RRSP for retirement income. Make no mistake! If you fail to contribute or to maximize your contributions as early as possible, the amount of RRSP money available to provide your retirement income will be reduced. You can look forward to a smaller retirement income as a result.

In addition, the higher the earnings rate, the better off you will be investing in an RRSP than investing outside an RRSP. That happens because your RRSP contribution gives you a larger sum to invest than you would have if you paid tax and invested only after-tax dollars.

The 1995 federal budget lowered the RRSP contribution limits. Moreover, the $8,000 RRSP overcontribution limit has been reduced to $2,000 beginning in January 1996. To phase in this reduction, your excess contributions can be left in your RRSP. However, to avoid the penalty, the new contributions must be reduced by the amount of your overcontributions that exceeds $2,000. This allows existing excess contributions to be retained until they can be deducted against new RRSP room, rather than forcing them to be withdrawn.

CONTRIBUTION RULES AND RRSP MECHANICS

Your contributions may be made each year and are deductible from income for tax purposes, within specific limits, in the year they are made or a subsequent year.

Contributions made in the first 60 days of the year are deductible in that year or in the immediately preceding year. Starting in 1991, unused deduction room for a given year, that is, up to the allowable contribution limit, may be carried forward for use in subsequent years.

Any income or capital gain arising in the RRSP is not immediately subject to tax, provided certain requirements are met. However, capital gains and dividends lose their special tax status when earned within an RRSP, and are fully taxed when withdrawn. Capital gains and dividends may therefore best be earned outside the RRSP. Tax is payable only when you withdraw funds or begin to receive a retirement income from the RRSP.

Who Can Contribute?

Anyone with earned income, as defined in the section "Earned Income" below, may contribute to an RRSP. However, since you must arrange to receive a retirement income from your RRSP by December 31 of the year you turn age 71, no further contributions can be made past this date. If you are 71 or older, you can still contribute to a spousal RRSP if your spouse is under age 71. If you have not yet reached age 71, but you are receiving an RRSP retirement income, you may continue to contribute to your own RRSP.

In its 1996 budget, the federal government proposed to lower the age limit from 71 to 69, beginning January 1, 1997. There is no reduction in the age limit if you attain age 70 in 1996, but if you turn age 69 or 68 in 1996, you will have to mature your RRSP by the end of 1997.

Children under the age of 18 may contribute to an RRSP, assuming they have "earned income" and meet RRSP rules. However, you may have trouble finding an issuer willing to enter into an RRSP contract with a minor. Some taxpayers have made contributions (for which no deduction is received) to their child's RRSP in order to split income with the child and reduce the family's overall tax bill. Depending on how long the funds are left in the RRSP and the child's tax rate at the time the funds are withdrawn, the tax deferral advantage may be sufficient to offset the increased tax cost. However, penalty taxes apply unless the child has deductible RRSP room. Moreover, there is no reduction of the penalty taxes on the $2,000 "excess contribution" limit unless the RRSP owner attained age 18 in a prior year.

Contribution Limits

Individuals Who Are Not Members of RPPs or DPSPs. The RRSP contribution limit for individuals who are not members of registered pension plans (RPPs) or deferred profit sharing plans (DPSPs) is 18 per cent of the prior year's earned income to a specific dollar maximum. For the years 1996 to 2002 inclusive, this maximum amount is set at $13,500.

For example, the maximum RRSP contribution for 1997 is 18 per cent of earned income in 1996 to a maximum of $13,500. To put it another way, if you want to contribute the maximum of $13,500 to your RRSP in respect of 1997, you need earned income in 1996 of at least $75,000.

Members of DPSPs or Money Purchase RPPs. For members of DPSPs or money purchase RPPs (those in which accumulated contributions and earnings in the plan are used at retirement to purchase the best possible pension), the RRSP contribution limit is 18 per cent of the previous year's earned income to the dollar maximums for the current year noted above, minus an amount called the "pension adjustment" (PA). The PA for these individuals is simply the total of all employee and employer contributions and reallocated forfeitures made in the previous calendar year to all money purchase RPPs and DPSPs (employees cannot contribute to DPSPs since 1991).

For example, assume that in 1996 your employer contributes $1,800 to your money purchase RPP and you contribute $1,600 to the plan. Your earned income in 1996 is $50,000 so your maximum RRSP contribution for 1997 is $9,000 (the lesser of $13,500 and 18 per cent of $50,000). From this you must deduct your PA from the previous year (1996) of $3,400 (RPP contributions of $1,800 and $1,600).

Thus, your allowable RRSP contribution in 1997 is $5,600 ($9,000 minus $3,400).

Members of Defined Benefit RPPs. For these individuals (who are guaranteed a specific pension by their RPP), the RRSP contribution limit is 18 per cent of the previous year's earned income to the dollar maximum for the current year, as noted above, minus a PA that reflects the value of accrued benefits under the RPP in respect of the previous year. (If the individual is also a member of a DPSP, the PA will also reflect the amount of the employer's contribution.)

Pension Adjustment for a Year

The PA is designed to ensure that pension plan (or DPSP) members in different plans, with similar incomes but different benefit rates, have equal access to tax assistance to help build their retirement income. The PA for a calendar year is used to determine the RRSP deduction limit for the following year.

For example, a member of a pension plan that provides generous benefits will have a relatively high PA, which will lessen the individual's ability to contribute to an RRSP. Many members of non-contributory defined benefit plans have found their ability to contribute to an RRSP restricted to $1,000 annually, starting in 1991. Less generous pension plans will result in a smaller PA and larger allowable RRSP contributions.

Employers must calculate PAs for each employee and report them as part of the T4 reporting process required by the last day of February. Once employees receive their T4, they can determine precisely their RRSP contribution limit for the following year. Revenue Canada also advises taxpayers of their RRSP deduction limit on their income tax assessment for the preceding year.

Earned Income

Your RRSP contribution limit is based on a percentage of your earned income while you are resident in Canada, which will include the following:

- salary or wages minus any allowable deductions from such income (other than RPP contributions, contributions to a retirement compensation arrangement, and deductions for a clergyman's residence);
- disability pensions paid under the Canada Pension Plan or Quebec Pension Plan, provided you were resident in Canada when you received the payments;
- income from royalties in respect of a work or invention of which the taxpayer was the author or inventor;
- income from carrying on a business, either alone or as a partner actively engaged in the business;
- net rental income, whether active or passive, from real property;
- payments from supplementary unemployment benefit plans;
- alimony or maintenance included in income for tax purposes (including that received by a common-law spouse), as well as reimbursements received by you of alimony or maintenance payments you paid;
- net research grants;

less the following:

- losses from carrying on business either alone or as a partner actively engaged in the business;
- net rental losses from real property;
- deductible alimony or maintenance payments, as well as reimbursements paid by you of alimony or maintenance payments you received;
- taxable capital gain from the disposition of qualified farm property included in the aforesaid business income.

Carry Forward Rule

If an individual contributes less than the maximum allowable amount to an RRSP in any particular year, the "unused RRSP deduction room" may be made up by contributions of more than the maximums otherwise permitted in later years. The amount that can be contributed in respect of unused RRSP deduction room may not exceed 3.5 times the RRSP dollar limit for the particular year.

Waiting until later years to make up deduction room carried forward may result in a tax cost and in many cases will result in a smaller accumulation in the RRSP by the time you retire. There also appears to be little point in delaying your contribution to a later year when you expect your tax rate will be higher, as your tax saving may be offset by the cost of giving up the tax shelter advantage that would have resulted from earlier contributions.

Withdrawals from an RRSP

RRSPs are intended to be held until retirement, at which point you would arrange an RRSP retirement income. However, there are no government restrictions against withdrawing funds from most RRSPs at any time. The amount withdrawn is included in income for tax purposes. If the withdrawal relates to a non-deductible excess RRSP contribution, an offsetting deduction may be available. You may withdraw funds tax-free to be used for a down payment on a principal residence under the Home Buyers' Plan. See "Special Situations" below.

Under a rule that became effective in 1986, you may withdraw any amount from your RRSP, if the plan so allows. Some plans require that you give up to one or two months' notice for withdrawal. Pre-1986 RRSPs will have to be amended by the issuer to allow such a partial withdrawal. The issuer of the RRSP is required to withhold tax at the following rates on any RRSP amount paid to you:

Amount	Canadian Residents Except Residents of Quebec (%)	Quebec Residents (%)
$5,000 or less	10	21
$5,001 to $15,000	20	30
Over $15,000	30	35

If you are withdrawing relatively large amounts from an RRSP or RRIF, you should consider making several separate withdrawals to lessen the withholding rate, and perhaps making withdrawals over several years to avoid a high marginal rate of tax on a portion of the funds.

Note that withholding is required on the portion of any RRIF payment in excess of the minimum annual amount required to be paid from a RRIF.

Spousal RRSPs

Any amount of your regular RRSP contribution can be contributed, in whole or in part, to an RRSP of which your spouse is the annuitant, whether or not your spouse makes an RRSP contribution in his or her own right (special rollover contributions cannot be made to a spousal plan). You should make the contribution directly to the trustee of the plan and have it receipted to you so you can prove that you made the payment.

Spousal RRSP contributions are extremely valuable for splitting income on retirement. For example, assume that your spouse will have few or no other sources of pension income, besides those from the government. If your spouse's marginal tax rate will be 25 per cent on retirement and yours will be 45 per cent, you and your spouse will have up to an extra 20 cents on every dollar of RRSP retirement income available. Expressed in percentage terms, your after-tax disposable income on the RRSP amounts after retiring could increase by over 36 per cent. In addition, your spouse will have income eligible for the tax credit on pension income when he or she reaches age 65.

Contributions to a spousal RRSP reduce the amount that you can otherwise contribute to your own RRSP. In other words, the total of amounts contributed by you to both plans is limited by your total deduction room available. You may not transfer amounts from your own RRSPs, RPPs, or deferred profit sharing plans (DPSPs) to a spousal RRSP, except on marriage breakdown or death.

If you are 71 years of age or older and have deduction room available, you may still make contributions to your spouse's RRSP if he or she has not reached age 71.

Within 60 days of the end of the year in which a taxpayer dies, it is possible for the legal representative of an estate to make a contribution to a spousal RRSP where the spouse is under age 71. This permits a deduction of such an amount on the deceased's final return of income. Please note that, as of January 1, 1997, the age limit of 71 is lowered to 69.

Withdrawals from a Spousal RRSP. A special rule prevents spouses from using a spousal RRSP to split income and hence reduce taxes. If your spouse receives funds from any of his or her RRSPs to which you have made a spousal contribution, from any commuted annuity from such a plan, or from any registered retirement income fund (RRIF) that receives funds from such a plan in excess of the minimum amount required to be paid from the RRIF, then an amount equal to the lesser of

(a) the amount received by your spouse; or
(b) the aggregate of contributions made by you to any plans on behalf of your spouse that were paid by you in the year of receipt of the funds and the two immediately preceding years (not including amounts previously added back to your income)

is added to your income and taxed in your hands. The excess, if any, of (a) over (b) is included in your spouse's income.

The following example will explain this rule. The following amounts are contributed to your spouse's RRSP:

Year	Amounts Contributed	
	By You	By Spouse
1	$2,000	—
2	—	$4,000
3	$1,000	—

If your spouse removes $4,000 from the RRSP at the end of Year 3, $3,000 is included in your income and $1,000 in your spouse's income. If your spouse had contributed the $4,000 to a separate plan in Year 2 and then withdrawn the $4,000 in Year 3, the entire amount would be included in your spouse's income, assuming you had not made a contribution to that particular plan.

This restriction on withdrawal applies regardless of the number of different RRSPs the spouse may have or whether funds have been transferred from a "spousal" RRSP to another RRSP to which no spousal contributions have been made directly. If your spouse receives funds from an RRSP to which only he or she contributed, the amounts do not have to be included in your income, even though you have made spousal RRSP contributions to other plans in the current year or the immediately preceding two years.

However, the rule does not apply on your death, or if you are divorced or separated and living apart from your spouse.

Locked-In RRSPs

Upon termination of employment, employees normally have the option of leaving their pension entitlements with their former employer, transferring them to a pension plan with their new employer, if the new employer is agreeable, or transferring them to a locked-in RRSP, which would be more restrictive than an ordinary RRSP and would not provide for withdrawals prior to retirement.

Typically, a locked-in RRSP will provide that, upon your retirement, you will have to use the RRSP funds to purchase an annuity, or a life income fund in Quebec. Certain provincial pension laws already require this treatment on transfers from RPPs to RRSPs.

Types of Contributions

You may contribute either cash or property to an RRSP, depending on the type of RRSP you have. The value of your contribution of property is the fair market value of the property at the time of contribution. You are deemed to have disposed of the property at fair market value when it is transferred to the RRSP and a gain or loss may result. Any gain must be included in income for tax purposes. Any capital loss, however, is denied to you and cannot be used to offset capital gains. Do not, therefore, sell "losers" to your RRSP. If you contribute a non-qualified investment (see below), the fair market value of that investment is included in computing your income for the year of contribution.

Borrowing for Your RRSP Contribution

Any interest paid on funds borrowed to make an RRSP contribution is not deductible for tax purposes.

You are likely better off borrowing to enable you to make a contribution than not contributing at all. It makes sense to borrow now to make a contribution rather than waiting several years to contribute in respect of unused deduction room carried forward, because you can begin sheltering income from tax in the RRSP much sooner than you otherwise would.

Transfers to and from an RRSP

Direct transfers of lump-sum amounts are generally allowed between plans on a tax-free basis, subject to a prescribed maximum. For example, tax-free transfers can be made directly from one RRSP to another RRSP, RRIF, or RPP. RRSP amounts can be transferred only by the issuer of the RRSP and only before the maturity of the plan.

The tax-free rollover of a retiring allowance into an RRSP is still permitted, subject to certain limits.

For service years after 1988 and before 1996, the limit is $2,000 per year of service. Up to and including 1988, this may be increased by $1,500 for each year for which no employer contributions to an RPP or DPSP are vested. To avoid tax being withheld on the retiring allowance, the employer can make the transfer directly to the RRSP.

Accumulated amounts in RRSPs may be transferred on a tax-free basis to another RRSP, to a RRIF, or to an RPP. The amounts must be transferred directly by the issuer of the RRSP. If you receive the amount directly, it must be included in your income for tax purposes and the tax-free transfer then cannot be made. After 1989, such transfers to your own RRSP, RRIF, or RPP can be made only before the plan matures.

You are allowed to make direct transfers of commuted annuity amounts and payments from a RRIF in excess of the required minimum payment or to an RRSP or another RRIF, or you may acquire any of the RRSP-type annuities. The annuity must provide for equal annual or more frequent payments, starting not later than one year after the transfer.

A "refund of premiums" (a defined term for RRSP purposes) received by a spouse or dependent person from the RRSP of a deceased person can also be transferred tax-free to your RRSP. The tax-free transfer of RRSP amounts to your spouse on marriage breakdown is also possible.

Penalties, Special Taxes, and Deregistration

Excess Contributions. When undeducted RRSP contributions exceed a certain limit at the end of a month, a 1 per cent penalty tax is imposed on the amount in excess of $2,000 ($8,000 before February 27, 1995) until this amount is withdrawn. Transition rules are provided for taxpayers with overcontributions on February 26, 1995, that do not exceed the $8,000 limit. These overcontributions can be retained in the RRSP without penalty and deducted as contributions for 1996 and subsequent years, until the limit is brought down to $2,000.

Foreign Investments. Generally you are allowed to invest 20 per cent of the cost of your RRSP investments in qualified foreign securities. If you exceed this level, your RRSP is subject to tax at the rate of 1 per cent a month on the excess amount invested in foreign securities for each month the excess remains in the RRSP. You may exceed the 20 per cent limit, within certain limits, if you make investments in eligible small businesses.

Non-Qualified Investments. If your RRSP acquires an investment that is not a qualified RRSP investment, the fair market value of the investment at the time of acquisition is included in your income in that year. In the year the RRSP disposes of the investment, you may deduct from your income the lesser of the proceeds of disposition and the amount previously added to income. Tax is payable at the top marginal rate by the RRSP on the income earned by the non-qualified investment.

If a qualified investment in your RRSP becomes a non-qualified investment, the RRSP must pay a special tax equal to 1 per cent of the fair market value of the investment at the time of acquisition for each month the investment retains its non-qualified status, or until the investment is disposed of by the RRSP, assuming the value of the investment was not included in your income.

Borrowing Money or Carrying on Business. If your RRSP borrows money at any point in the year, tax is payable by the RRSP on all its income each year until the borrowed funds are repaid. An RRSP is a trust and therefore is subject to tax at the maximum personal rate in your province of residence. If the RRSP carries on a business at any time during the year, the resulting business income is subject to tax at regular trust rates.

RRSP as Collateral for a Loan. If any of your RRSP property is used as collateral for a loan, the fair market value of the property used as collateral is added to your income in that particular year. When the RRSP property ceases to be used as collateral, an amount equal to the amount previously added to income less any losses suffered on the loan transaction may be deducted from income. If, however, the RRSP is a depository-type plan, it will be subject to deregistration should any of the RRSP be pledged, assigned, etc., in which case the entire amount in the plan is included in your income for tax purposes and there is no way that the plan can be subsequently reinstated.

Deregistration. RRSPs can be deregistered for a variety of reasons, in which case the fair market value of all the assets of the particular plan are included in income for tax purposes in the year the plan is deregistered. However, issuers will structure your RRSP to prevent it being deregistered in most circumstances (i.e., the contract or arrangement you have with the issuer will prohibit actions that would result in deregistration).

An RRSP will automatically be deregistered if you do not arrange a retirement income to be paid by December 31 of the year you turn age 71 (69, beginning January 1, 1997). The plan is effectively deregistered on the first day of the following year and its full value included in income therefore in the year you turn age 72 (70, beginning January 1, 1997). Some plans provide for an automatic annuity purchase if no other retirement income is arranged, but an annuity may not suit your retirement income needs.

RRSP INVESTMENTS

Interest, Dividends, or Capital Gains in Your RRSP

If all your investments are held inside an RRSP, your investment strategy should be to maximize your return over the long term. All amounts received from RRSPs are taxed at full rates. Capital gains and dividends earned in an RRSP lose their identity and are not eligible for preferential tax treatment.

If you have investments both inside and outside RRSPs, the rules of thumb are somewhat different.

First, interest-bearing investments should be held in the RRSP, not outside, as interest income is taxed at full rates outside your RRSP.

Second, preferred shares or common shares that pay dividends should generally be held inside an RRSP, but not if you are then forced to hold interest-bearing securities outside the RRSP.

One other observation is possible concerning the balance of your RRSP investment portfolio. Generally, the younger you are, the more heavily you may want to weight your portfolio in favour of equities. Since you are investing for the long term, you can take advantage of the expected higher return over this period and you are able to weather the ups and downs of the stock market. However, the closer you are to retirement, the more heavily your RRSP (and non-RRSP investments as well) should be weighted toward less risky investments such as interest-bearing securities to protect your accumulated capital.

Canada Deposit Insurance

You should ascertain if your RRSP investments are covered by the Canada Deposit Insurance Corporation (CDIC), or other comparable deposit insurance programs generally established on a provincial basis for deposits made with credit unions and caisses populaires. Qualifying investments include savings and chequing accounts, and guaranteed investment certificates and term deposits that are redeemable within five years. The insurance does not apply to foreign currency deposits, such as U.S.-dollar savings accounts or U.S.-dollar GICs or mutual funds.

The maximum insurance coverage provided by CDIC is $60,000 per customer per member institution, while the coverage available to members of credit unions and caisses populaires varies by province and is at least equal to the CDIC coverage. If you have RRSPs with more than one member institution, whether directly or through a self-directed plan, your coverage is multiplied.

Similarly, if you have a self-directed RRSP that holds investments from various member financial institutions, each of these investments will be covered separately. CDIC insurance on your RRSP is separate from CDIC insurance on investments you hold personally, which in effect doubles your maximum coverage at one institution to $120,000.

Types of RRSPs

RRSP investment vehicles are available in the following major categories:

- insurance-type, where you contract to pay a certain amount, usually periodically, in return for a retirement income of a certain size paid periodically;
- depository RRSPs, where your deposits are made directly with the issuer; and
- RRSP trusts, the most common being self-directed RRSPs where you make the investment decisions.

Insurance companies sell RRSPs that are similar to and competitive with RRSPs sold by other financial institutions. Life insurance RRSPs are usually not protected under the CDIC, although they are self-insured by the insurance industry.

Self-Directed RRSPs

Self-directed RRSPs generally provide convenient monthly reporting from one source and facilitate the spreading and varying of risk. As investment objectives change over time, the make-up of a self-directed investment portfolio can be updated, providing maximum flexibility.

SPECIAL SITUATIONS

Home Buyers' Plan

The 1994 federal budget continued the Home Buyers' Plan, effective March 2, 1994, but only for first-time home buyers who apply after March 1, 1994. An individual is a first-time home buyer if neither the individual nor the individual's spouse owned a home and lived in it as his or her principal place of residence in any of the five calendar years beginning before the time of the withdrawal. Individuals, who are able to participate in the Home Buyers' Plan only once, may withdraw up to $20,000 from their RRSPs to buy a home without having to pay tax on the withdrawal. The withdrawals are to be repaid to the home buyer's RRSP in instalments over a maximum period of 15 years. For example, if an individual withdrew $15,000 from an RRSP under the Home Buyers' Plan, the scheduled annual repayment would be $1,000 per year ($15,000 divided by 15 years).

The 15-year repayment period begins in the second calendar year following the calendar year in which the withdrawal is made. A qualifying home must generally be acquired before October 1 of the calendar year following the year of the withdrawal. A participant may elect to have a repayment made in the first 60 days of a year treated as having been made in the preceding year.

If, in any year, the individual decides not to repay the scheduled amount, or decides to repay only part of it, the amount that is not repaid will be included in the individual's income for the year and, consequently, will be subject to tax.

You should restore the funds taken from your RRSP as quickly as possible to maximize your retirement income.

You are allowed to repay more than the scheduled annual repayment in any year. This results in a lower outstanding balance and lower scheduled annual repayments for the remainder of the pay-back period.

A special rule denies a tax deduction for contributions to an RRSP that are withdrawn within 90 days under the Home Buyers' Plan. Contributions within the 90-day period are not considered to be withdrawn except to the extent that the RRSP balance after the withdrawals is less than the amount of such contributions.

Even if your RRSP permits maximum withdrawal, it may not be advisable because potential investment of tax-free income in the RRSP will be forgone until the funds are repaid.

Marriage Breakdown

On the breakdown of a marriage, funds may be transferred from one spouse's RRSP or RRIF to the other spouse's RRSP, RRIF, or RPP on a tax-deferred basis. The attribution rules, under which income from property transferred from one spouse to the other is taxed in the hands of the transferor, not the recipient, do not apply to such an RRSP transfer. In addition, the rules discouraging the collapsing of spousal RRSPs do not apply on the breakdown of a marriage.

In order not to be taxed, payments made as a result of marriage breakdown from one person's RRSP to the RRSP of the person's spouse or former spouse must be pursuant to a decree, order, or judgment of a competent tribunal or a written separation agreement.

RRSPs and Non-Residents

The tax consequences of becoming a non-resident can be extremely complex. Deciding how to deal with your RRSP should be considered in concert with the many other financial and tax decisions you must make at that time. In very general terms, tax is withheld from many types of payments originating in Canada and made to residents of another country. The other country also may tax the "payment", but most give credit for any Canadian taxes already paid (i.e., withheld at source). The Canadian tax treatment of RRSP amounts generally depends on whether the RRSP has matured, and also on your new country of residence.

Creditor Access to Your RRSP

The courts have decided that creditors may gain access to a bankrupt's RRSP to settle debts. Only some insurance-type RRSPs offer any creditor protection, but recent case law may weaken that protection in certain cases. However, creditors cannot gain access to life annuity payments, and they may have trouble seizing term-certain annuity payments or the funds in a RRIF. Switching your RRSP to an insurance company shortly before you declare bankruptcy probably will not offer any protection, since the bankruptcy laws see through these types of transactions.

RRSPs on Death

The tax treatment of RRSP amounts on the death of the annuitant depends on whether the RRSP had matured and on the beneficiary. A spouse receives the most generous treatment. To ensure that RRSP amounts go to the intended beneficiaries with as little trouble as possible, you should name specific RRSP beneficiaries in the RRSP contract or in your will.

If the RRSP has not matured, generally the fair market value of all RRSP property is included in the income of the deceased in the year of death and taxed accordingly in the final income tax return before it is distributed to beneficiaries of the deceased.

However, there are two exceptions. First, if a spouse (including a common-law spouse) is named as beneficiary, the plan is essentially transferred to the spouse on a tax-deferred basis.

Second, a "refund of premiums" is not included in the deceased's income. A refund of premiums, which includes all accumulated income, is defined as either

- any amount paid to the deceased annuitant's spouse from the RRSP, even if the spouse was not specifically named as a beneficiary; or
- if the annuitant had no spouse at the time of death, amounts paid to dependent children or grandchildren named as beneficiaries, who were financially dependent on the annuitant.

A spouse, or physically or mentally infirm child, may transfer a refund of premiums to his or her own RRSP or RRIF on a tax-deferred basis in the year of the annuitant's death or within 60 days of the end of that year. In addition, a spouse or a mentally or physically infirm child may purchase a life annuity or term-certain annuity to age 90 with the refund of premiums. Other children in receipt of a refund of premiums may set up an annuity that runs until they reach 18 years of age.

The legal representative of the deceased's estate may elect for either the spouse or, if there is no spouse, qualifying dependants to receive a refund of premiums.

Somewhat similar rules apply to RRIFs. If the deceased's spouse is the beneficiary, the plan is essentially transferred to the spouse on a tax-deferred basis, and the spouse receives all future payments.

MATURING YOUR RRSP

The decisions to be made before your RRSP matures are not automatic. Careful consideration must be given to your retirement goals, the amount of money that will be required to achieve those goals, and the time at which the money will be required. The tax impact of arranging for your retirement income should also be examined. It is necessary to weigh the RRSP retirement income options carefully. Competent professional advice is recommended when planning for your retirement income.

Maturity Options

RRSPs must be matured before December 31 of the year the annuitant turns age 71 (69, beginning January 1, 1997). Before 1986, RRSPs could not be matured until the annuitant turned age 60. You should ensure that the terms of RRSPs in existence before 1986 are changed to allow for early maturity.

"Maturing" an RRSP simply means arranging to receive a retirement income from accumulated RRSP funds. In the case of some insurance RRSPs, it is simply the date you begin receiving the stipulated RRSP income, assuming you have not notified the issuer otherwise.

With non-insurance RRSPs, there are essentially three maturity options. First, you can arrange to receive an annuity, of which there are several types. Second, you can transfer the accumulated RRSP funds into a RRIF from which a periodic retirement income is received. Third, you can collapse the RRSP and receive a lump sum after paying the relevant tax.

You can choose any or all of the options and have as many different types of annuities and RRIFs as you want. This flexibility allows you to arrange the type of retirement income you need to suit your expected income requirements. For example, you might consider collapsing a portion of your accumulated RRSPs to finance spending in the early years of your retirement, perhaps for extended travel, although this can also be accomplished with a RRIF. You also probably want to build in a certain amount of inflation protection by transferring some of your RRSP funds to a RRIF and/or indexed annuity.

Even after choosing your retirement income options, RRSPs remain particularly flexible, as you can switch from option to option with relative freedom. For example, you can switch a RRIF to another issuer to earn a better return. As well, you can have as many RRIFs as you like. You can also withdraw any amount from any RRIF at any time, although a minimum amount must be withdrawn from each RRIF each year. You also may be able to commute RRSP annuities, depending on the terms of the contract, in which case the commuted amount becomes taxable. However, amounts withdrawn from a RRIF in excess of the required minimum amount and commuted annuity amounts may be directly transferred on a tax-deferred basis to other annuities or a RRIF, or even to an RRSP if you are under age 72 (70, beginning January 1, 1997). You also may be able to buy an impaired health life annuity from some life insurance companies, which provides for larger payments if you can establish that your life expectancy is considerably shorter than normal.

You do not have to acquire an annuity or RRIF from the issuer of your RRSP.

Shop around for the best rates on the options you want, and consider using an annuities broker or other professional advisor to search for the best rates and make arrangements for you.

It is extremely important that you do not wait until the last minute to arrange maturity of your RRSP, i.e., December 31 of the year you turn 71 (69, beginning January 1, 1997).

If you miss the deadline, all accumulated funds in your RRSP are included in income in the year following the year you turn 71 (69, beginning January 1, 1997), with no recourse for correcting your oversight.

Early Maturity

Maturing your RRSPs early can be expensive in terms of reduced income. Try to delay maturing your RRSPs until you absolutely must, or mature only a portion of your accumulated RRSP funds at any one time. If you are age 65 or older, RRSP retirement income qualifies for the pension income tax credit. See Chapter 5.

RRSP Annuities

There are essentially two types of annuities – life and term certain. Under a life annuity, the periodic payments, which you must receive at least once a year, continue until you die. The amount payable is based on the average life expectancy for someone your age and on current interest rates, among other factors. Term-certain RRSP annuities are payable to age 90, or to the year your spouse turns age 90. Payments cease after your ninetieth year and are based primarily on current interest rates.

The table on page 83 illustrates the monthly income that a $50,000 investment will produce when invested in various ways at particular ages. The figures were supplied by the Polson Financial Group, Retirement Income Specialists, a Toronto-based RRIF/annuity broker.

Monthly incomes shown commence one month after purchase date. The listed incomes are subject to change as interest rates fluctuate, and represent an average of the highest-yielding plans at September 6, 1996.

When considering your retirement income options, remember that payments in the early years for indexed annuities are considerably lower than those for level payment annuities, but are much higher in later years. It is extremely important that you carefully assess your income requirements over the long term before committing yourself to any of the options.

Registered Retirement Income Funds (RRIFs)

RRIFs have a number of advantages over annuities:

- The inflation protection factor can be better controlled than for indexed annuities since the size of annual payments is extremely flexible.

- Unusual income requirements in any year can be taken care of since you can withdraw any amount from a RRIF at any time, provided you withdraw at least the minimum amount.
- You can control the investments made in the RRIF, which generate the retirement income. (Of course, bad or risky investing could dissipate your RRIF funds.)
- Your estate benefits because substantial amounts can remain in the RRIF, especially during the early years of its existence.
- You can convert amounts in a RRIF to a life annuity at any time, but the conversion cannot be reversed unless the life annuity is purchased through an RRSP and you are under age 71 (69, beginning January 1, 1997).

	Single Life Annuity (10-Year Guarantee)		Joint Life Annuity (10-Year Guarantee)	Term Certain to Age 90	RRIF (First Year's Income Only)
Age at Purchase	Male	Male & Female	Male & Female	Minimum at Female	8% Interest
60	$388	$364	$345	$337	$139
61	393	368	348	340	144
62	398	373	352	344	149
63	404	377	355	348	154
64	410	382	359	353	160
65	416	388	364	358	167
66	423	393	368	363	174
67	429	399	373	370	181
68	436	405	379	376	189
69	444	412	384	383	198
70	451	419	391	391	208
71	458	426	397	400	308

A RRIF resembles an RRSP. Funds are invested by the issuer, or the RRIF can be self-directed. Different plans may hold different types of eligible investments, which are broadly similar to those allowed for RRSPs. All amounts in a RRIF remain tax-sheltered until paid out, and investment performance affects the overall value of the plan.

A minimum amount must be paid out from each RRIF each year to the annuitant and be included in the annuitant's income for tax purposes.

As a result of the 1992 federal budget, the rules were changed to permit RRIF withdrawals to continue for the lifetime of the RRIF holder (or his or her spouse), instead of ceasing at age 90. The table on page 85 compares the newer minimum withdrawal percentages to those under the former rules.

The current rules apply to all RRIFs to which funds are transferred after the end of 1992. For most RRIFs purchased before the end of 1992, or consisting exclusively of funds transferred from pre-1992 RRIFs ("qualifying RRIFs"), the previous minimum payment percentages will continue to apply for those up to age 77. However, the lower minimum payment percentages for those above age 78 will apply to all RRIFs, regardless of the date of purchase.

At any point, you may withdraw any amount from any or all of your RRIFs, provided that you withdraw at least the minimum amount from each RRIF each year. However, by withdrawing large amounts, you will be reducing the size of payments in future years. Withholding tax is payable on any excess withdrawn over the minimum amount that must be withdrawn in the year. The tax withheld becomes a credit against your tax payable for the year.

Minimum Annual Withdrawal (% of RRIF Assets)

	Former Rules[1]	Current Rules (%)	
Age	(%)	General	Qualifying RRIFs
71	5.26	7.38	5.26
72	5.56	7.48	5.56
73	5.88	7.59	5.88
74	6.25	7.71	6.25
75	6.67	7.85	6.67
76	7.14	7.99	7.14
77	7.69	8.15	7.69
78	8.33	8.33	8.33
79	9.09	8.53	8.53
80	10.00	8.75	8.75
81	11.11	8.99	8.99
82	12.50	9.27	9.27
83	14.29	9.58	9.58
84	16.67	9.93	9.93
85	20.00	10.33	10.33
86	25.00	10.79	10.79
87	33.33	11.33	11.33
88	50.00	11.96	11.96
89	100.00	12.71	12.71
90	N/A	13.62	13.62
91	N/A	14.73	14.73
92	N/A	16.12	16.12
93	N/A	17.92	17.92
94 or older	N/A	20.00	20.00

1 The factors in this column are equal to $1/(90 - x)$, where x is equal to the age of the annuitant or the annuitant's spouse, as the case may be.

Virtually everyone should consider putting at least a portion of his or her RRSP in a RRIF on retirement because of the flexibility of the plans.

The surviving spouse of a RRIF annuitant who dies after 1990 becomes the annuitant under the fund, provided that the parties have previously agreed to the ongoing payments, or the legal representative of the first annuitant consents and the carrier of the fund undertakes to make payments to the surviving spouse. Payments will then continue to the spouse, and be taxable in the spouse's hands only as each payment is received.

Collapsing Your RRSP

The third RRSP retirement option is distasteful to many because of the tax consequences.

If you collapse an RRSP, the entire amount in the particular plan must be brought into income and taxed in that year, often at the highest personal tax rate. See "Withdrawals from an RRSP", above.

If your retirement plans include moving to a foreign country and thus becoming a non-resident of Canada, you may be able to save on Canadian taxes by first establishing your non-resident status and then collapsing your RRSP. Non-resident withholding tax will apply to the funds withdrawn from your RRSP, but this will likely be at a lower rate than the rates outlined above for residents of Canada, particularly if you become a resident of a country with which Canada has a tax treaty providing for a specially reduced rate of withholding.

There is no withholding of provincial tax if you are a non-resident and have collapsed your RRSP after you ceased being a Canadian resident.

If you remain resident in Canada, need to use RRSP funds,

and want to save tax, average your income by collapsing RRSPs over several years. With only three tax brackets, however, the maximum tax rate is difficult to avoid. Not everyone will save tax by collapsing RRSPs over several years.

Besides paying tax at a high marginal rate when you collapse an RRSP, you also lose the tax deferral that is still available in the RRSP, in a RRIF, or even in an annuity. This probably is of little concern if the RRSP is collapsed to satisfy immediate cash requirements.

The major advantage of collapsing an RRSP is that funds can be made available in an amount to suit your needs in the early years of retirement. There does not even have to be an excessive tax cost if you are under age 71 and do not mature your other RRSPs until you absolutely must. However, a similar result can be achieved with a RRIF, possibly at lower cost, and it can generally be done more easily.

CHAPTER SEVEN

Investing for the Future

Capital Gains Exemption

The $100,000 capital gains exemption, which had existed since 1985, was abolished on February 22, 1994. So that individuals who had not exhausted their deduction would not be penalized, they could have filed "an election" with their 1994 income tax returns. However, special rules have been provided for the cancellation, amendment, or late filing of an election.

Meanwhile, the $500,000 capital gains exemption for "qualified small business corporation shares" and "qualified farm property" is still available.

Special Rules for the February 22, 1994, Election

Even if the election to use the $100,000 exemption was for 1994, it could be made for the 1995 taxation year in the following situations:

- where the fiscal period of a business included February 22, 1994, and ended after 1994, the election could be made on or before April 30, 1996, on eligible capital property (usually intangible) used to carry on that business;
- for personal trusts, the election could be filed on or before March 31, 1996, or, in other words, the calendar year following

the year in which the taxation year of the trust including February 22, 1994, ended.

Despite the April 30, 1995, deadline, and the other deadlines mentioned above, you can file an election *in the two years following* these dates. However, a penalty will apply.

Moreover, you can usually amend a previously filed election before 1998. Again, however, there is a penalty.

The penalty is 1/3 of 1 per cent of the taxable capital gain (or additional gain) multiplied by the number of late months (in the first situation) or by the number of months between the filing due date of the election and the date of the amended election (in the second situation).

Generally, you can also cancel a previously made election before 1998. Written notice to that effect must be sent to Revenue Canada. No penalty is then applicable.

According to the basic rule applicable to any election made for capital property owned on February 22, 1994, if such an election has been made in respect of a property, the property is deemed to have been disposed of for proceeds equal to the designated amount, without exceeding its fair market value at February 22, 1994, and reacquired for the same designated amount. As a means of discouraging individuals from indicating an amount higher than the fair market value at February 22, 1994 (to generate higher gains than the gains accrued to that date), an adjustment mechanism is provided when the designated amount *exceeds 110 per cent of the fair market value* of the property at February 22, 1994.

In this situation, the reacquisition cost of the property for the elector is instead equal to the fair market value less the excess of the designated amount over 110 per cent of the fair market value. In addition, individuals who have filed an excessive election cannot amend or cancel the election, contrary to the above information.

For example:

Fair market value (FMV) of property at February 22, 1994		$10,000
Less: Amount designated in February 22, 1994, election	$12,000	
110% of above FMV (110% × $10,000)	$11,000	
Excess	$ 1,000	(1,000)
New adjusted cost (ACB) base of property		$ 9,000

If the excess had been more than $10,000, deduction of this amount in calculating the ACB would have resulted in a negative ACB. Therefore, the ACB would have been increased to zero, thereby resulting in a capital gain in 1994 for which a capital gains exemption could not be claimed.

Eligible Capital Property and Flow-Through Entities

Special rules exist when you have filed an election in respect of *eligible capital property* (usually intangible) used to carry on a business and on interests in *flow-through entities* (defined below). Instead of increasing the tax cost of the property by the capital gains realized at the time of the election, these gains are recorded in an account called an "exempt gains balance" (for eligible capital property) and an "exempt capital gains balance" (for flow-through entities). As the capital gains are realized on the properties in the future, they could be tax-exempt up to the amounts in these balances.

For purposes of this rule, a flow-through entity includes, among other things, a mutual fund corporation, a mutual fund trust, or a partnership. You have until December 31, 2004, to reduce your respective "exempt capital gains balance" to zero. If the balance is not reduced to zero by that date, the balance amount will then be added to the adjusted cost base of the interests still held in the entity. Also, when you cease to hold an interest in a flow-through entity at any given time, your exempt capital gains balance related to the entity for the taxation years beginning after that date is reduced to zero.

Non-Qualifying Real Property

Where you have made an election on *non-qualifying real property*, the portion not eligible for the capital gain (i.e., the portion accrued between March 1, 1992, and February 22, 1994) is not considered when calculating the capital gain for purposes of the election. The adjusted cost base and the capital cost following the deemed reacquisition are therefore reduced by this non-eligible portion, whereas there is no change for purposes of capital cost allowance.

Property Owned on December 31, 1971

Where you have made an election on *non-depreciable property* owned by you on December 31, 1971, the result of using the transitional rules is that the capital gain accrued before 1972 is not taxed. When the property is actually sold, the act specifies that the property will not be deemed to have been owned on December 31, 1971. However, when the election is made on *depreciable property* owned on December 31, 1971, you are deemed to have owned the property continuously since December 31, 1971, until the time of eventual disposition (after February 22, 1994).

$500,000 Exemption

The deduction permitted in computing your taxable income for a year for qualified farm property and qualified small business corporation shares represents the lesser of the three following amounts:

- the unused portion of maximum capital gains exemption;
- the annual gains limit for the year; or
- the cumulative gains limit at the end of the year.

The unused portion of the maximum capital gains exemption corresponds to the amount of exemption available over your lifetime, less the portion used up in previous years. *The annual gains limit for the year* equals the amount of the capital gain for the year from the disposition of eligible small business corporation shares or qualified farm property, less deferred capital losses and allowable business investment losses.

This annual gains limit must be calculated on an annual basis. However, your position must also be considered on a cumulative basis since the deduction applies over your lifetime. Hence, for a particular taxation year, the cumulative results of previous years must also be taken into account. This is what is meant by the *cumulative gains limit.*

Cumulative Net Investment Losses

Since 1988, net capital gains eligible for the capital gains exemption (CGE) have been reduced by all cumulative net investment losses (CNILs) deducted in computing income for taxation years after 1987. The purpose of this reduction is to prevent you from using your CGE to offset capital gains and, in the same year, offsetting your other income with investment losses that may well represent interest paid on money borrowed to invest in shares that generated the exempt capital gain. Your CNIL at the end of a year is the amount by which your accumulated investment expenses exceed your accumulated investment income.

Basically, your investment expenses consist of the following items that have been deducted in computing your income for the 1988 and subsequent taxation years:

- Deductions claimed with respect to property that will yield interest, dividends, rent, or other income from property. Such deductions include interest, safe deposit box rental, other carrying charges, capital cost allowance (CCA), and so forth.

- Carrying charges, including interest, with respect to an interest in, or a contribution to, a limited partnership (unless you are the general partner) or any other partnership where you are not actively engaged in the business of the partnership (unless you carry on a similar business).
- Your share of a loss (except allowable capital losses) of any partnership described above.
- Fifty per cent of your share of deductions attributed to a resource flow-through share or relating to Canadian exploration and other resource expenses of a partnership where you are not actively engaged in the business.
- Any loss for the year from property or from renting or leasing real property (including a MURB) owned by you or a partnership, not otherwise included in the investment expenses listed above.
- The amount by which net taxable capital gains realized between March 1, 1992, and January 22, 1994, that are not eligible for the CGE (e.g., a portion of gains realized on disposition of a vacation or investment property you own in addition to your principal residence) are offset by net capital losses of other years that are deducted by you in the year.

Your investment income for a year essentially consists of the following items that are included in computing income for the year:

- Interest, taxable dividends, rent, and other income from property (including recaptured depreciation in respect of items generating income from property).
- Your share of the income (including recaptured depreciation but not including taxable capital gains) from most limited partnerships or other partnerships where you are not actively engaged in the business of the partnership (unless you carry on a similar business).

- Income (including recaptured depreciation) for the year from property or from the renting or leasing of real property owned by you or a partnership not otherwise included.
- Fifty per cent of recovered exploration and development expenses included in income.
- The income portion of certain annuity payments, other than those from an income-averaging annuity contract or an annuity purchased pursuant to a deferred profit sharing plan.
- Net taxable capital gains realized between March 1, 1992, and February 22, 1994, that are not eligible for the CGE (e.g., a portion of gains realized on disposition of a vacation or investment property you own in addition to your principal residence).

Whether your capital gains qualify for the CGE or not, you are still able to deduct the interest paid on funds you borrow for investment purposes. The CNIL rules are concerned only with the calculation of your CGE. You need not be concerned with them if you have previously exhausted your CGE.

The interest expense on funds you use to carry on an unincorporated business or profession does not enter into the CNIL calculation.

Your net investment loss is not calculated on an investment-by-investment basis, nor on an annual basis, but rather on a cumulative and pooled basis after 1987 for all your investment assets. Carrying charges associated with one security may therefore reduce your capital gains exemption available to offset a taxable capital gain realized on the sale of another security. The CNIL rules do not erode your CGE, but they can delay your use of all or part of it until your cumulative investment income exceeds your cumulative investment expenses. If you intend to use your exemption in 1996, your CNIL balance at December 31, 1996, will be taken into consideration. If you have a positive CNIL balance, you may wish to take certain steps to eliminate it.

If you own a company, consider receiving, prior to December 31, 1996, dividends or interest from the company to reduce or eliminate the CNIL balance.

Since there are a number of factors to consider, you should consult your professional tax advisor.

After having discussed the method of calculating the $500,000 capital gains exemption, it is important to be aware of the conditions small business corporation shares and farm property must satisfy in order to be eligible for the exemption.

Qualified Small Business Corporation Share

In order to qualify for the exemption, the share must, at the time of disposition, be owned by you (or a person or partnership related to you) and must be *shares of the capital stock of a small business corporation.*

By "small business corporation" is meant a Canadian-controlled private corporation of which *all or substantially all of the fair market value of the assets is used principally in an active business carried on primarily in Canada* (other than a specified investment business and a personal services business). The assets may also be shares in one or more small business corporations connected with the corporation or a bond, debenture, or similar obligation issued by such a connected corporation.

The shares must also satisfy two additional requirements in order to qualify for the $500,000 exemption: one relating to the *retention of the shares* and the other relating to the *use of the assets.*

First, the holding period requirement provides that throughout a period of 24 months immediately preceding the disposition, the share *must not have been owned* by any person or partnership other than yourself or a person or partnership related to you. Newly issued shares can also meet the test; the requirement is not that you have owned the shares for 24 months, only that *no one else has owned them.*

As for the active business asset requirement, an extended definition of a small business corporation is used.

Throughout the 24-month holding period, more than 50 per cent of the fair market value of the corporation's assets must have been used in an active business.

At the *time of disposition* of the shares, all or substantially all (in Revenue Canada's view 90 per cent or more) of the fair market value of the assets must have been used in such a business (this is the general definition for a small business corporation). Assets considered to be used in an active business consist of:

- assets used principally in an active business carried on primarily in Canada by the corporation or a related corporation; and
- certain shares or debt of connected corporations that are small business corporations.

Qualified Farm Property

The disposition of qualified farm property entitles an individual to a capital gains exemption of $500,000. This is not an additional exemption added to the exemption already commented on concerning qualified small business corporation shares or on other property. These deductions can be used at the same time provided that *the total capital gain exempted does not exceed $500,000.*

The $500,000 exemption on qualified farm property was first introduced in 1985. However, certain changes have been introduced on June 17, 1987, to the definition of the term "qualified farm property".

The qualified farm property must be owned by you, your spouse or a partnership, if the interest in such partnership is an interest in a family farm partnership of you or your spouse. This last rule enables you or your spouse to qualify for the exemption in situations where the family farm partnership owned the property that was disposed of.

The terms *family farm partnership* and *family farm corporation* (mentioned below) mean an entity that carried on the business of farming in Canada in which it used more than 50 per cent of the fair market value of all of its property and in which the farmer, or the farmer's spouse or child was actively engaged on a regular and continuous basis.

Qualified farm property can be:

- real property (land or building) that has been used in the course of carrying on the business of farming in Canada (but see below);
- a share of the capital stock of a family farm corporation of the individual, the individual's spouse, or any of the individual's children;
- an interest in a family farm partnership of the individual, the individual's spouse, or any of the individual's children; and
- eligible capital property (usually intangible) used in a farming business, to the extent that the disposition of such property creates a capital gain under section 14.

Additional comments are necessary concerning the applicability of the capital gains exemption for the *real property* mentioned above. It must have been used in the course of carrying on the business of farming in Canada by:

- the individual;
- a beneficiary of a trust related to the person from whom the trust acquired the property;
- the spouse, a child, the mother or father of the individual; or
- a partnership or a family farm corporation in which any one of the above three classes have an interest.

The real property must meet other requirements to qualify for the exemption. For at least 24 months preceding the disposition, the real property must have been owned by one of the persons mentioned above. One of the following conditions must also be met:

- for at least two years, the gross revenue from the farming business earned by any one person mentioned above must exceed the individual's net income from all other sources; or
- through the 24-month period, the real property must have been used by a partnership or a *family farm corporation* (mentioned above) in the course of carrying on the business of farming in Canada.

The purpose of the gross revenue criterion and the requirement that the real property be used in a farming business is to allow the exemption only to individuals for whom farming is the main activity.

However, a real property acquired before June 18, 1987, that would not meet the above criteria could qualify for the exemption if the requirements prior to this date were met; it must have been used for farming in the year of disposition or in at least five years (not necessarily consecutive) during which the property was owned by any person mentioned above.

Other Capital Gains and Losses

The following discussion applies to all taxpayers, but particularly to those who will be taxable on their capital gains or who have incurred capital losses from the disposition of other property.

Allowable capital losses, other than "business investment losses" (see below), offset taxable capital gains in the year. Any unused allowable capital losses can be carried back to the three preceding years, or be carried forward indefinitely to offset taxable capital gains in future years. You may choose the amount of loss carryovers to use and the year in which you use them. Do not apply losses so that you end up with unused dividend tax credits or other deductions or tax credits.

A loss on transfer of property to a corporation controlled by you or your spouse must be deferred until your shares in the corporation are sold. A loss on transfer of property to your RRSP, your RRIF, or your spouse's RRSP is denied completely.

Therefore, consider selling the property to realize the loss, and then transferring or reinvesting the proceeds, taking care to avoid the superficial loss rules (see below).

Settlement Date. Remember that a disposition of shares through a stock exchange is deemed to take place at "settlement date". For Canadian exchanges, settlement date is three business days after the trading date. This means the last trading date in 1996 is December 24. However, if the transaction is a cash sale (payment made and share certificates delivered on the trade date), you have until December 31, 1996, to make the trade.

Superficial Loss. You cannot claim a capital loss on an asset you really intend to continue to hold. This rule also applies if the assets are acquired by your spouse, a corporation controlled by you, or any other affiliated person. Thus, where property is sold at a loss and the same asset or "identical" assets are purchased within 30 days before or after the disposition, and the repurchased asset is still held at the end of the 30th day following the original disposition, a "superficial loss" results. The person acquiring the replacement asset adds the loss to his or her cost base and the seller of the asset is denied the loss. The rule does not apply if the assets are acquired by your children or parents.

Identical Properties. Capital properties of a similar kind are subject to special rules covering "identical properties". Stocks of the same class, or bonds of identical characteristics of the same corporation are "identical properties". These assets are "pooled", and lose their specific identities.

If 200 shares of a stock are purchased for $8 per share and, subsequently, 100 shares are purchased for $11 per share, the tax cost of the shares is considered to be $9 per share ($2,700 / 300). If the 100 shares purchased for $11 are sold the next day at the same price, you will have a capital gain of $2 per share, which will result in $150 (three-fourths of $200) being included in income.

Business Investment Losses

A business investment loss is the loss incurred on the disposition of shares in, or the debt obligations of, a small business corporation (as defined above). A business investment loss may be used to reduce income from other sources.

Shares or debt must be disposed of to a person with whom you deal at arm's length. Shares also will be considered disposed of if the corporation is bankrupt (or, in some circumstances, if it has ceased to carry on business), and debt will be considered disposed of if the debt is established to be uncollectible.

Three-fourths of the business investment loss, the "allowable business investment loss" (ABIL), is treated in the same manner as a non-capital loss, such as a business loss. This means that you must deduct the allowable portion from all sources of income in the current taxation year. Unused losses may be carried back three years and forward seven years. Income in the loss year must be reduced to zero before these losses can be carried backward or forward, with the result that personal tax credits are lost. However, you do have a choice how much of a loss carryover you want to claim in a carryover year. After the seven-year carry-forward period, unused allowable business investment losses become ordinary capital losses and may be carried forward indefinitely.

A taxpayer's business investment loss for a taxation year after 1985 is treated as an ordinary capital loss to the extent of any claims made under the lifetime capital gains exemption in previous years. In addition, any capital gain realized is not eligible for the capital gains exemption to the extent of any business investment losses realized by the taxpayer in prior years after 1984.

Reserves for Proceeds Not Yet Due

If a capital asset is sold, giving rise to a capital gain, and the full amount of the proceeds is not due by the end of the year, a part of the capital gain may be deferred by claiming a reserve for the proceeds not yet due. The amounts brought into income each year are treated as ordinary capital gains. The includable amounts will be based on the inclusion rate in the year the reserve is brought into income (not the inclusion rate in the year the asset was sold). You may claim less than the maximum available reserve in any year. If you do so, however, you cannot claim a larger reserve in the next year.

As a rule of thumb, the reserve must be brought into income and taxed over a maximum period of five years, as stipulated in the act. Also, a ten-year reserve, instead of a five-year reserve, is allowed on the transfer of farm property, shares in a family farm corporation, or shares in a small business corporation to your child, grandchild, or great-grandchild (resident in Canada).

Dividends

Dividends are grossed up by 25 per cent, and the dividend tax credit is 16.67 per cent of the cash amount of dividends received. The following example shows how a top-bracket taxpayer with federal tax payable in excess of $12,500 is taxed on a $1,000 dividend received in 1996.

Cash dividend	$1,000
Gross-up	250
	1,250
Federal tax (29%)	363
Dividend tax credit	(167)
	196
Surtaxes	16
Provincial tax (assume 55%)	108
Total tax	$ 320
Amount retained after tax	$ 680

An individual with no dependants and with only dividend income could receive approximately $23,800 of dividends in 1996 without paying federal tax, depending on the province of residence.

Interest

In the past, interest income accrued in a year but not received in that year could be reported every three years.

However, for interest-bearing investments acquired after 1989, interest income must be reported annually.

If you own pre-1990 investments on which interest accrues but is not payable, you may still report the interest income every three years as opposed to annually. (See Chapter 3.)

Investing in Tax Shelters

Many upper-income Canadians have discovered the hard way that the "quality of investment" aspect of a shelter is by far the most important element, overshadowing all other considerations, including immediate tax savings. Receiving a deduction for the money you put into a tax shelter is no consolation if you end up losing your money because the investment is a bad one. If you are considering investing in a tax shelter, you should obtain professional advice before committing your funds and future state of mind to these high-risk investments.

Limited Partnerships. Generally, the investment tax credits and losses claimed by limited partners are limited to the extent that their investment in the partnership is at risk. These "at-risk rules" do not apply to certain limited partnerships in existence on February 25, 1986. The amount at risk for the first purchaser is generally the adjusted cost base of his or her partnership interest at the end of the year plus his or her share of the current year's income of the partnership. This amount is reduced by any amount owing to the partnership and any guarantee or indemnity provided to protect the limited partner against the loss of his or her investment. Moreover, when allocating losses of a partnership or withdrawing funds results in a negative cost base, the negative amount is considered a capital gain of the partner in the year it becomes negative. Despite the strict rules, limited partnerships frequently offer a good way of arranging financing and limiting risk.

Mineral Exploration and Oil and Gas Shelters. With flow-through shares, the various deductions and tax credits associated with oil and gas drilling and mineral exploration flow through directly to shareholders.

Multiple-Unit Residential Buildings (MURBs). Since 1994, MURBs have been treated in the same way as other rental properties owned by persons not actively engaged in the real estate business. Thus, capital cost allowance can be used only to reduce rental income to zero, but not to create a loss deductible against other income.

Canadian Films. In 1987, you could claim your total investment in a certified Canadian film production as capital cost allowance over two years. The applicable rate is 30 per cent per year, calculated on a declining balance basis (the half-year rule does not apply). A further deduction is granted when annual income from Canadian film productions is sufficient. The change is effective generally for investments acquired after 1987 and before March 1, 1996. In 1994, new rules were introduced that curtail perceived abuses relating to these investments. The benefit of capital cost allowances on certified Canadian film allocations to produce losses is thus reduced by any convertible debt that has been put in place to reduce the impact of the "at-risk" rules.

These rules have been replaced by a system of refundable credits to Canadian film producers with no possible flow-out to investors. The new system is applicable to films produced after February 29, 1996.

Farming as a Tax Shelter. Depending on the crop or product raised, and the market for it, farming may be a viable tax shelter. However, several rules in the tax law, including a mandatory inventory adjustment, make it more difficult to create losses from farming to offset income from other sources. As well, most taxpayers will be subject to the restricted farm loss rules, which limit deductible losses in a year to $8,750 ($5,000 for taxation years commencing before 1989).

Farming may also be attractive as a tax shelter because of the $500,000 capital gains exemption available for gains on qualifying farm property. You don't necessarily have to be a full-time farmer to take advantage of this exemption.

Provincial Tax Shelters. Many provinces provide incentives to encourage investment in certain areas or industries. For example, some provinces have stock savings plans that provide for tax credits, and some also have venture capital plans to encourage investment in small to medium-size companies.

CHAPTER EIGHT

Owner-Managed Private Companies

If you own your own business, you may wonder whether to operate in corporate or unincorporated form. Traditionally, the Canadian income tax system has favoured incorporated Canadian small businesses. The calculations for income and deductions remain essentially the same as for an unincorporated business. (You should refer to the various sections in this book for details regarding income, deductions, autos, and so forth.) There are some differences, however, in the structure of corporate taxation, and in planning opportunities through corporations.

Corporation Defined

A corporation is an artificial person created by law. A corporation will have the following characteristics:

- It is a separate legal entity, which has ongoing existence and the ability to contract, i.e., buy, sell, employ, borrow, lend, and own property.
- It must act through individuals.
- Ownership is represented by shareholders, who also may be employees.
- Profits are distributed by dividends, which are taxed in the hands of the shareholders.
- It is a separate taxable entity and must file income tax returns and pay taxes.

Corporate Taxation – Basics

If you run your business as a sole proprietorship, you include the income from the business on your personal tax return, as discussed in Chapter 2. A corporation, on the other hand, is a separate taxable entity. The corporation must file its own tax return and pay its own tax instalments. You include income from the corporation on your personal tax return only when you receive distributions from your corporation in the form of salary, dividends, interest, or some other payment.

Similar to the individual rate structure, the corporate structure varies according to the province where the corporate income is generated. In addition, however, the tax rate varies based on the type and amount of income.

The basic federal income tax rate for corporations is 38 per cent. This rate is decreased to 28 per cent on income earned in Canada to accommodate provincial and territorial taxation on such income. A further deduction from the basic tax rate is available for income generated from manufacturing and processing (M&P) activities performed in Canada. The M&P deduction is 7 percentage points, and thus reduces the federal corporate rate to 21 per cent.

There is also a federal surtax of 4 per cent of the net federal rate, which increases the federal tax rate for income earned in a province from 28 per cent to 29.12 per cent without the M&P deduction, and to 22.12 per cent with the M&P deduction.

Special tax treatment is provided if your company is a Canadian-controlled private corporation (CCPC).

Basically, a CCPC is a resident Canadian corporation, controlled by Canadian residents (other than public corporations). Generally, this control will exist if such Canadian residents hold at least 50 per cent of the voting rights in the company.

However, this is not always the case. When a person has any

direct or indirect influence that, if exercised, would result in control of the corporation in fact, he or she is considered to have control of the corporation. For example, a person who holds 49 per cent of the votes of a corporation may be considered to control it where the balance of the votes is widely dispersed among employees of the corporation or is held by a person who could reasonably be considered to act in accordance with the wishes of the person holding the 49 per cent voting interest.

A CCPC is eligible for a federal tax rate reduction (the small business deduction – SBD) on up to $200,000 of active business income annually. (If the corporation's tax year is less than 12 months, this amount must be prorated.)

The federal tax rate reduction may apply to a lesser amount, or even be completely cancelled, if taxable income of the corporation and associated corporations for the previous year exceeded $10 million.

The annual $200,000 limit must be shared by "associated corporations" to prevent taxpayers from abusing this SBD by forming several corporations to multiply the $200,000 eligible for the reduced rate. Generally, associated corporations are corporations controlled by the same person or group of persons. Thus, it is not possible to set up several corporations and obtain the benefits of the SBD on $200,000 of income for each of them. It also is important to note the requirement that the income be "active business income". If you incorporate your investment portfolio, you will not qualify for the small business deduction because the income generated will not be active business income.

The federal small business deduction (SBD) is 16 percentage points.

There is no M&P deduction for income eligible for the SBD. Therefore, if your company is a CCPC generating income from an active business in Canada, the federal corporate tax rate will be 12 per cent for the first $200,000 of taxable income. When you include the 4 per cent federal surtax (calculated on 28 per cent), the federal income tax rate is 13.12 per cent. For income in excess of the $200,000, the normal corporate tax rates noted above will apply.

In addition to the federal corporate tax, all provinces also impose income taxes. The provincial tax rates vary from nil to 17 per cent, depending on the province, whether there is an M&P deduction, whether there is a small business deduction, and whether the province grants a tax holiday (often for new corporations). Combined federal and provincial corporate income tax rates, therefore, vary considerably.

A federal tax is imposed at a rate of 0.225 per cent on a large corporation's capital employed in Canada in excess of $10 million. With such a large threshold, most small businesses are not subject to this Large Corporations Tax (LCT). The 4 per cent surtax that corporations are required to pay can, however, be used to offset LCT liability. The LCT cannot be deducted in computing income subject to income tax.

Tax Deferral

For small companies, the combined federal-provincial corporate tax rate is between 18.12 and 23.12 per cent, depending on the province. In Quebec, a tax rate of 18.87 per cent is in effect for the 1996 calendar year. If you compare these rates with those for individuals shown in Chapter 13, you see that the small company rates are significantly lower.

If you operate your business in unincorporated form, you will include the income from the business in your personal tax return as it is earned. Thus, you will pay tax on your business income at your personal marginal tax rate. If you incorporate your business, you initially pay only the corporate tax rate. You will not pay individual tax on the corporate earnings unless you receive distributions in the form of salary, interest, or dividends and you are therefore able to defer the personal tax on the portion of earnings retained in the business.

For example, if you earned $1,000 of pre-tax income, you would pay about $530 in individual taxes at the top marginal rates. That would leave $470 for reinvestment in the business. If the $1,000 were generated by a corporation eligible for the SBD, the maximum corporate tax would be about $189, leaving $811 for reinvestment. No individual tax would be due until earnings were distributed to shareholders. Thus, in this example, as much as $341 ($530 minus $189) of tax might be deferred.

Setting Up the Corporation

Generally, you can transfer your business assets to a corporation without any tax consequences, subject to certain restrictions. In return, the corporation must issue shares to you. You may choose to have part of your investment in the corporation in the form of debt rather than shares. By holding some debt, you have the opportunity to draw earnings out of the corporation as interest, which is tax-deductible to the company, as well as drawing earnings out as dividends.

Taxation of Distributions from the Corporation

When you receive payments from the corporation, the tax treatment depends on the nature of the payment. Salary you receive as an employee of your corporation is fully includable in your income in the year of receipt. If you have financed your company partly by lending the company money, any interest income is fully includable in your income. If you have leased assets to the corporation, lease payments paid to you would be included in your income when received, and so forth. All such payments would be deductible in calculating the corporation's income. You could benefit from deferring the tax on these payments insofar as you can obtain a tax deduction for the corporation before you have to pay the individual tax on the payments. There are some restrictions on this deferral ability regarding delays for accrued payables.

It also may be possible to achieve limited deferral through the payment of salaries or bonuses. In such a case, for the corporation to obtain a deduction in the year the salaries or bonuses were accrued, these amounts must be paid within 180 days after the corporation's year end. When they are paid, you include them in your taxable income. However, if the corporate year end is after July 5 (i.e., a July 31 year end or later), the amounts can be paid in the following calendar year, but within 180 days after the corporation's year end. This provides about six months of tax deferral benefit.

Integration

Although you may own most or all of the shares of a corporation, both you and the corporation are separate taxpayers. The corporation pays income tax when profits are earned. When the after-tax profits are distributed from the corporation as dividends, they are included in your income and the corporation does not receive a deduction. Consequently, profits generated through a corporation are taxed twice, once when earned by the corporation and again when distributed as dividends to the shareholders.

To alleviate this double taxation of income earned through a corporation, the corporate and individual tax systems are integrated. This integration is accomplished by grossing up the dividend received by the shareholder to approximate the amount earned before tax at the corporate level. A tax credit is then granted in an amount designed to give the shareholder a credit for the amount of tax already paid by the corporation.

Accordingly, if you receive a dividend distribution from your corporation, include an additional 25 per cent of the dividend in your income (to gross-up the dividend). After you calculate your federal income tax (before calculating the surtax of 8 per cent), you take a dividend tax credit equal to two-thirds of the amount by which you grossed-up the dividend payment. For Quebec taxes, the dividend tax credit is 44 per cent of the dividend gross-up.

For example:

Dividend received	$100
Dividend gross-up (25% × $100)	25
Taxable income	$125
Federal tax at 29% (maximum)	$ 36.25
Dividend tax credit (2/3 × $25)	(16.67)
Federal tax before surtax	$ 19.58
Federal surtax (8% × $19.58)	1.57
Total federal tax	$ 21.15
Provincial tax (55% assumed rate × $19.58)	10.77
Total individual tax on dividend	$ 31.92

The integration system is rough justice designed to approximate an individual's receiving dividends from a corporation that has enjoyed the small business deduction. To achieve perfect integration, the federal and provincial combined corporate rate must be 20 per cent, there must be no surtaxes, and the individual must have a provincial tax rate of 50 per cent. Under these conditions, there will be no difference between earning business income through a corporation or directly, as demonstrated in the following example (which assumes a taxpayer in the highest tax bracket).

	Income Earned Directly	Income Earned Through a Corporation
Corporate income		$100
Corporate tax		20
After-tax profits		$ 80
Individual income		
Business profits	$100	
Dividend		$ 80
Dividend gross-up (25% × $80)		20
Taxable income	$100	$100
Federal tax at 29%	$ 29	$ 29
Dividend tax credit (2/3 × $20)	0	(13.33)
Provincial tax at 50%	14.50	7.83
Total individual tax	43.50	23.50
Corporate tax	0	20.00
Total tax on $100 income	$ 43.50	$ 43.50

To the extent that the tax rates differ from these hypothetical rates, there will be differences in total taxes paid, depending on whether the income is earned directly by an individual or through a corporation. If the corporate tax rate and/or individual tax rates are lower than these hypothetical rates, the total tax paid on income earned through the corporate structure is likely to be less than the total tax that would be paid if the income were earned directly by the individual. To the extent the corporate tax rates are higher than for a small business corporation, there will be a shortfall in relief from double taxation.

Advantages and Disadvantages of Incorporating Your Business

The trade-offs between the corporate and unincorporated structures depend to a great extent on the nature of your activities and the income generated. To determine the tax differential, you must review the differences between the corporate and individual tax rates for the province in which the activities are carried out. In many cases, however, it will be advantageous to have a corporate structure.

Generally, the tax and non-tax advantages to incorporating your business include:

1. Limited Liability. Because the corporation is a separate legal entity, individual shareholders are not responsible for corporate debts or other liabilities. This may not be an advantage for a small business, because it is common for lending institutions to request personal guarantees on loans to such a corporation. However, your liability remains limited for such things as lawsuits, unless you are personally negligent.

2. Tax Savings or Deferral. As mentioned above, there may be tax savings opportunities and tax deferral opportunities. The savings or deferral opportunities are of particular value to a business that will be investing to expand. The extent of these opportunities depends on the comparative corporate and individual tax rates in the particular circumstances, as well as on the nature of the income earned.

3. Income Splitting and Estate Planning. There are income splitting and estate planning opportunities available through a corporate structure that are not available with an unincorporated business. Some of these are reviewed in Chapters 4 and 10.

4. Levelling of Income. It is possible to achieve a levelling of personal income through control of salary and dividends to avoid high- and low-income periods, particularly in a business where profits fluctuate from year to year.

5. Pension Plans. A shareholder who is also an employee of the corporation may participate in the company's registered pension plan (RPP). A sole proprietor may not participate in an RPP. There also are other types of fringe benefits such as group term life insurance plans and group sickness or accident insurance plans, which may be available to you as an employee of your company, but are not available if your business is unincorporated.

6. Capital Gains Exemption. The corporate structure permits access to the capital gains exemption on the sale of shares of the corporation running the business. The $500,000 capital gains exemption is available to holders of shares of a small business corporation (which is not available if the business is unincorporated). This exemption includes the regular $100,000 capital gains exemption on other capital properties, which was abolished on February 22, 1994.

A "small business corporation" is a CCPC that uses all or substantially all (90 per cent and more, expressed in terms of fair market value, according to Revenue Canada) of the fair market value of its assets in an active business carried on primarily in Canada. The shares of a Canadian holding company also qualify if substantially all its assets are shares or debt of other small business corporations. To qualify for the $500,000 exemption, the corporation must be a small business corporation at the time of the sale and the shares must not have been held by anyone other than the seller, or related persons, within the 24 months preceding the sale. In addition, throughout the 24-month period, more than 50 per cent of the fair market value of the assets of the corporation must be used in an active business carried on primarily in Canada for the $500,000 exemption to be available. (For a holding company, the qualifying tests for small business status are more stringent.)

Disadvantages of the corporate structure include:

1. Losses. A corporation is unable to use losses to offset income generated by the individual. If you generate losses through an unincorporated business, you may use these losses to offset income from other activities. Because the corporation is a separate entity, neither the income nor the losses flow directly to your individual tax return. As a result, you cannot use these losses to offset other types of income. If the corporation generates income in other years, the losses may offset such other income of the corporation (business losses of the corporation for a given year may be carried back three years and forward seven years to offset other income of the corporation). Note that, if your corporation is generating a loss, the reported loss can be adjusted by reducing your salary payments and substituting dividends.

2. Costs of Incorporating. There are additional costs to setting up and maintaining a corporation that you would not have with an unincorporated business. Such costs include the initial expenses of preparing the legal documents and taxes such as provincial capital taxes. Ongoing costs include filing forms such as tax returns, holding meetings, maintaining corporate records, and so forth.

3. Capital Taxes. A few years ago, the federal government introduced a special tax similar to the capital tax system that has existed in some provinces for years. Because this tax is payable only when the capital used in Canada by the corporation exceeds $10 million, the federal capital tax liability is usually eliminated or substantially reduced for small corporations.

The Quebec capital tax rate is 0.64 per cent. An exemption is available for the first three taxation years of a newly incorporated business with paid-up capital less than $2 million. Nevertheless, a minimum capital tax of $250 must be paid each year.

Planning with Your Owner-Managed Corporation

There are several aspects of planning that should be reviewed if you have incorporated your business. It is important to keep in mind non-tax factors while developing your plan, however. You need to consider your cash needs, and the cash needs of the company. In addition, you must review all your other sources of income, and your position regarding investment income, capital gains, and investment losses. All these factors should be considered when you are reviewing your tax planning for your company.

Payment of Investment Income

One aspect you may want to review is your position under the cumulative net investment loss (CNIL) rules discussed in Chapter 7. If you have cumulative net investment losses, you may want to receive interest or dividend income from your corporation. This income would be netted against any investment losses to reduce the amount of your CNIL. In this manner, the potential restriction of your $500,000 capital gains exemption can be avoided.

Spousal Salaries

You also may want to consider the payment of a salary to your spouse or other family members. It is necessary that the person actually perform some services for the company, that there be a bona fide employer–employee relationship, and that you be able to support the salary as reasonable. A salary generally will be considered reasonable if a reasonable businessperson would have paid the salary under similar circumstances and it is commensurate with the value of the responsibilities assumed and the services performed.

Under these conditions, the corporation will obtain a deduction for the salary payment, and you will have achieved additional income splitting. This salary payment also may open the opportunity for increased contributions to retirement savings plans for that family member.

Salary/Dividend Trade-Offs

One of the interesting areas of planning for the owner-managed corporation is the determination of the appropriate split between salary payments and dividend payments for the owner-manager.

Salary reduces corporate income tax payable, but the salary then is subject to personal tax. Although a dividend does not reduce corporate tax, the dividend tax credit means less personal tax is paid than on salary income. In theory, it is not supposed to matter whether you draw a salary or a dividend provided the company's taxable income (and that of all associated companies, pro-rated for any tax years less than 12 months) is not more than $200,000.

Similarly to the example above regarding integration, this theory is effective only when the combined federal and provincial corporate rate is 20 per cent, there are no surtaxes, and the individual is in a 29 per cent federal tax bracket in a province imposing tax at 50 per cent of the federal rate. In such a case, if 100 per cent of after-tax corporate income is distributed, the total tax would be identical whether it is distributed as salary or as dividends. (For every $100 of corporate income the numbers would be identical to those in the previous example.)

The theory is fine, but the system does not work exactly in the way it was intended. While in many provinces drawing a salary and maximizing RRSP contributions will be preferable to drawing a dividend, this is not true for all provinces, nor for all types of business activities.

It is generally advisable to withdraw at least as much from the company as possible until the net amount of tax you pay is equal to the tax the company would have paid had you not withdrawn the funds.

Depending on your particular circumstances, the best way to do this may be taking all salary, or a combination of salary and dividends. You can lend funds back to the company, and at any time in the future the company can repay the loan to you on a tax-free basis.

The above comments, however, assume that the corporation (and all associated companies, etc.) generates active business income of $200,000 or less. Thus, the full amount of taxable income would be eligible for the small business deduction. If there is taxable income in the corporation in excess of $200,000, the small business deduction does not apply to this excess, and the corporate tax rate will be considerably higher. Accordingly, it is generally advisable to keep the taxable income of the corporate group at or below $200,000. The most common way of achieving this goal is through salary payments to you as the owner-manager.

This salary will be included in your taxable income in the year of receipt. Recall, however, that in certain cases you may obtain the deduction for the corporation in a year earlier than the year in which you actually receive the payment. There may be a slight deferral advantage to leaving income in the corporation, but the total tax is likely to be higher than if salaries were paid.

Another aspect of the salary payment is that it is important to maximize the amounts that you can contribute under the Canada/Quebec Pension Plan and RRSPs. These plans have contribution limits based on your earned income for the year. As a result, even though the corporate income may be less than $200,000 without additional salaries or bonuses, you may want to pay enough salary to yourself to maximize your contributions to such plans, providing you have not fully used your pension amount in a company pension plan.

It is important to note that the contribution limit for RRSPs for a given year is now based on the income earned in the preceding year. Consequently, your earned income in the preceding year must be at least $75,000 in order to contribute the maximum amount ($13,500) to your RRSP for the current year.

It must be noted that for salaries to be deductible by the corporation, they must be "reasonable". What constitutes a reasonable salary is generally a question of fact. However, as a rule the tax authorities do not question the payment of a salary or bonus to a shareholder manager provided payroll tax withholdings are paid.

Selling Your Business

If your business is unincorporated, and you are contemplating its sale, you can in most cases transfer the assets to a corporation and then immediately sell the shares of the corporation to take advantage of the $500,000 capital gains exemption.

If your business is already incorporated, but does not qualify as a small business corporation, it may be possible to purify the corporation by removing non-qualified assets from the company. With careful planning, this removal could be effected on a tax-free basis. Generally, however, the purification process should begin long before a sale is being contemplated. There is a provision that could deny the capital gains exemption on a sale of shares of a corporation if appreciated assets have been removed from the corporation on a tax-free basis as part of the sale process.

If you are expecting to sell the shares of your company, you could consider accumulating income in the company to increase the gain. This must be done carefully, however, because, to maintain the small business corporation status, substantially all (90 per cent and more, according to Revenue Canada) the assets, expressed in terms of fair market value, must be used in carrying on the corporation's business. As a result, you could not accumulate earnings in the corporation and use those earnings to buy passive investments if such investments would constitute more than 10 per cent of the total fair market value of the corporate assets at the time of sale (or more than 50 per cent for the preceding 24 months, as discussed earlier). However, you might be able to use the earnings to reduce the corporation's debts and other liabilities.

When you are negotiating the sale of your business, the buyer may prefer to buy the assets of the company, rather than buying your shares. This provides the buyer with tax write-offs that would be unavailable if the buyer purchased the shares. On your part, the preference will be for a sale of the shares because of the capital gains exemption and the possibilities for spreading exemptions within your family if you previously have organized the share structure to permit ownership by your spouse and children (see the discussion following).

There is room for negotiation. If the disposition qualifies for the $500,000 capital gains exemption, you should be able to negotiate a deal with a purchaser that permits both of you to share the tax benefits from your expanded capital gains exemption.

Corporate Planning and Your Family

It may be possible to reorganize the capital structure of your company to permit ownership by your spouse and children should you so desire. Properly planned, a reorganization of the capital structure may provide both income splitting and estate planning opportunities. Arranging for share ownership by a spouse and children also could provide for a reduction in tax if the company is sold, particularly if the corporation is a small business corporation, since each family member would be entitled to the $500,000 capital gains exemption.

Reorganizing share capital does have its pitfalls and you should not proceed without proper advice.

As you can see, tax planning for your business may provide opportunities for income splitting, tax deferral, increasing your capital gains exemption, estate planning, and retirement planning. Attempting to pull all these factors together into a complete and thorough plan is a complex task. Since the presentation here is necessarily restricted, you may wish to consult your professional tax advisor for personalized planning in this area.

CHAPTER NINE

You and Your Car

This chapter highlights the principal tax rules affecting the business use of automobiles. However, in view of the complexity of these rules, professional advice still will be required to deal adequately with many situations.

TAX ASPECTS FOR EMPLOYEES: EMPLOYEE-PROVIDED AUTOS

Allowances and Reimbursements You Receive

If you own your own car, your company may provide you with various types of benefits in respect of the time you use the car for business or for personal purposes.

One approach is for your employer to pay you an "automobile allowance". This may be calculated to cover only the business-related costs of owning and operating the auto, or may be intended as part of your remuneration package (in excess of business-related costs). Allowances are treated by your employer in one of two ways. If the allowance is not a reasonable amount for business-related purposes, it must be reported on your T4 slip as employment income for the year. In this case, you generally may deduct a portion of the expenses incurred if you operate the auto for business use, provided you are required by contract to use the auto in the course of your employment and meet certain other criteria. Employers must also add the 7 per cent GST (and the 6.5 per cent Quebec Sales Tax [QST], if applicable) to the taxable benefit in respect of the use of an automobile.

Alternatively, if the employer pays you for business use of an automobile, and if the amount is a reasonable allowance for that purpose, generally the employer should not report such an allowance as taxable income.

An allowance will be considered "reasonable" only if it is directly related to the number of business kilometres driven in a year and if no reimbursement is received for expenses related to the same use.

To make the first condition possible, you may be expected to provide your employer with detailed records for business kilometres driven. Second, the allowance will still be considered reasonable even if there is a reimbursement for the cost of additional commercial insurance for the car, parking, tolls, and ferries, as long as the allowance is determined without reference to these expenses.

In addition, an allowance will be considered "reasonable" only if the rate per kilometre is reasonable.

Your employer may pay you at a higher rate without reporting it as taxable income to you if the higher rate is "reasonable". However, your employer is limited in the deductibility of the allowance paid to you and may not be willing to incur a non-deductible expense. As well, Revenue Canada has stated that it considers that, generally, the prescribed rate for the employer's deduction is representative of a reasonable per-kilometre allowance. In any event, you should keep records to indicate the cost of operating your car in case you are called upon to support the allowance.

You may want to consider the alternative of having the

allowance treated as taxable remuneration. If this is done, you will be permitted to deduct at least a portion of the costs of operating the auto for business purposes if you meet all the criteria. In many circumstances, this may work out to your advantage. Moreover, you may be able to claim GST (and QST) rebates on your deductible expenses. For more details, see Chapter 12.

Specific reimbursements of direct costs incurred in the operation of your car in your employer's business (e.g., gas used for identifiable business travel) are not allowances and are not considered in calculating your taxable income.

Deducting Expenses from Your Income

Eligibility. You may be allowed to claim various deductions for the ownership and operating costs of your auto related to its use in the course of your employment. To be eligible for these deductions, you must not be in receipt of a tax-free allowance, and you must be required by your terms of employment (technically your contract of employment, which need not be written) to pay your own travel expenses. You also must be required to work away from your employer's place of business or in different places on an ordinary basis. A prescribed form (T2200 for federal purposes and TP-64.3 in Quebec) must be signed by your employer to confirm that these conditions have been met and must be filed with your tax return. If you are claiming expenses, any payment received from your employer in respect of ownership of the car must be a taxable allowance, and any reimbursement of operating expenses by your employer must be subtracted from any deduction claimed in relation to the same expense.

Salespeople selling property or negotiating contracts for their employers, and remunerated by commissions related to the volume of sales made or the contracts negotiated, may deduct auto and other expenses only up to the amount of such commissions, unless travelling expenses are the only type of expenses being claimed.

If you qualify to deduct auto expenses, you may deduct the business portion of the actual costs of ownership and operation, subject to the limitations discussed below for autos costing more than $24,000 ($20,000 for autos acquired before September 1, 1989).

Deductions for Owned Vehicles

If you own the car you use for business purposes, you are permitted capital cost allowance (CCA) on the total cost, but not exceeding one of the following amounts (hereafter the "maximum prescribed cost") for autos acquired:

- after December 31, 1990: $24,000 plus GST and provincial sales tax applicable on $24,000;
- after December 31, 1988, and before January 1, 1991: $24,000, including provincial sales tax;
- before January 1, 1989: $20,000, including provincial sales tax.

If you acquired the car from a non-arm's-length person (a related person), the cost for CCA purposes is the least of the maximum prescribed cost, fair market value immediately before the disposition, and the transferor's undepreciated capital cost (UCC) immediately before the transfer.

Upon disposition of an auto, the terminal loss and recapture rules will cease to apply where the cost is in excess of the maximum prescribed cost.

For CCA purposes, the cost of each car that is less than $24,000 is included in class 10. CCA is allowed at 30 per cent (15 per cent in the year of acquisition) on a declining-balance basis.

When the cost of a car, without the applicable taxes, is $24,000 or more, it is included in a separate pool within class 10.1. CCA for a class 10.1 asset is also allowed at 30 per cent (15 per cent in the year of acquisition) on a declining balance basis. However, you may claim CCA at 15 per cent in the year of disposition of a class 10.1 car.

For instance, if the cost of your car purchased on October 1, 1996, is $35,000, because of the half-year rule, applicable in the first year of ownership, you may claim 15 per cent of the maximum prescribed cost in that year. In the second year and the following years, you may claim 30 per cent of the excess of the maximum prescribed cost over CCA previously claimed. In the year in which the car is sold there will be no assets in the class at year end and no CCA can be calculated. However, one-half of the depreciation (CCA) that would have been allowed in the year of sale if the car were still owned at year end will be deductible.

You also are permitted to deduct interest on a loan that is directly related to the purchase of the car. The interest deduction is limited to a maximum average of $300 per month ($250 for autos acquired before September 1, 1989) for the period that the loan is outstanding.

The reduced amounts of depreciation and interest calculated as above are further reduced in proportion to business use.

Deductions for Leased Vehicles

If you lease your car, you may deduct the least of

- the actual lease cost;
- $650 per month plus GST and provincial sales tax applicable on $650 for leases entered into after 1990 (a fixed amount of $650 or $600 per month for leases entered into before 1991 and before September 1, 1989, respectively);
- the actual lease cost times the maximum prescribed amount and divided by 85 per cent of the manufacturer's suggested list price. For leases entered into before 1991, provincial sales tax must be added to the suggested list price.

For example, for an Ontario resident, if your car's manufacturer's suggested list price is $34,000 and the monthly lease payment under a lease entered into on October 1, 1996, is $700, the three alternatives will be $700, $748, and $669 ($700 x $27,600/85 per cent of $34,000). The maximum deduction will be $669. This example is not necessarily representative of the circumstances that will apply to this price range of car.

Reductions for Personal Use

Deductible ownership or lease costs as calculated above must be reduced further by multiplying them by the ratio of business kilometres to total kilometres.

Your deduction for operating costs (fuel, repairs, and maintenance) is also limited in the same proportion. The same rule holds true when calculating your eligible GST rebate (QST rebate for repairs and maintenance only).

Purchase Assistance

Your employer may be willing to assist you in the purchase of your car, for example, by providing you with an interest-free (or low-interest) loan. In this case, the forgone interest is considered a taxable benefit at government-prescribed rates of interest, which may change every quarter. Accordingly, your taxable earnings are increased by the amount of the loan outstanding times the prescribed interest rate for the period the loan is outstanding. However, this interest amount is considered an expense and you may deduct a portion of the deemed interest payment using the rules discussed above.

Because you probably would have paid more than the prescribed rate if you had borrowed the money from a bank, but the cost to the employer (including lost investment income) is likely to approximate the prescribed rate, such a loan may be one of the best ways of receiving a real benefit at a relatively low tax cost.

TAX ASPECTS FOR EMPLOYEES: COMPANY-PROVIDED AUTOS

If your company provides you with a car, you could be required to include several amounts in taxable income. These amounts include a standby charge (a notional charge for making the car available to you), any benefit you receive for operating expenses paid by your employer for personal use, and taxable allowances. As mentioned earlier, the value of the benefits added to your income is subject to GST (and QST, if applicable), which is payable by your employer. Employers are required to report the GST (and QST, if applicable) as a taxable benefit on their employees' T4s (Relevé 1 in Quebec). Specific reimbursement of out-of-pocket expenses (gasoline, parking, etc.) directly related to business use would not be included as a taxable benefit. However, it may be to your advantage to understand how your employer calculates the taxable amount. In some cases (and assuming you have a choice), you may prefer to own your own vehicle and receive an allowance, rather than using a car provided by your employer.

Standby Charge

You must include in your taxable income a "standby charge", which is designed as a rough measure of the benefit to you of having the car available for personal use. This charge is calculated differently, depending on whether the car is owned or leased by your employer.

Owned Vehicles. If the auto is owned by your employer, the standby charge is 2 per cent of the original cost of the car (including GST and provincial sales tax) for each month the car is available to you (24 per cent for a full year). This 2 per cent is calculated on the full cost of the car, regardless of whether this cost is in excess of the maximum prescribed cost.

This standby charge may be reduced if you use the car all or substantially all for business (interpreted by Revenue Canada as 90 per cent or more) and your personal use is under 1,000 kilometres per month.

In this case, the standby charge is calculated as follows:

$$\text{Standby charge otherwise calculated} \times \frac{\text{kilometres for personal use in the year}}{1{,}000 \times \text{number of months in the year in which the car is available to the employee}}$$

For instance, if your personal use is only 200 kilometres per month and this equals 5 per cent of the total use, you will be taxable on only 20 per cent (2,400 km/12,000 km) of the standby charge otherwise calculated. You should note, however, that commuting to your employer's office is considered personal (not business) use of the car.

An optional method is available for calculating the standby charge if you are employed principally in selling new or used cars.

The standby rules apply to members of a partnership as if they were employees.

Leased Vehicles. The standby charge included in your income for autos leased by your employer is two-thirds of the lease cost (including GST and provincial sales tax) and any amount included in the lease cost for repairs and maintenance, but excluding any amount included for insurance. (You should note that the insurance amount is included in operating costs for the purpose of determining any operating benefit, but is excluded to establish the benefit resulting from GST and QST, if applicable.) This charge is calculated on the full lease cost paid by your employer, whether or not the amount in respect of which your employer may claim deductions is the full cost.

It may be better for you if your employer leases the car rather than owns it. Two-thirds of the lease payment may work out to less than 24 per cent of the cost that would be chargeable if the employer owned the vehicle. And, there is greater flexibility, in that some service costs can be included in the lease contract and hence be taxable benefits to you only to the extent of two-thirds.

Where your personal use is less than 10 per cent and less than 1,000 kilometres per month, this standby charge also may be reduced as discussed under "Owned Vehicles", above.

Reimbursements to Your Employer

If you reimburse your employer for part of the cost of the auto, the standby charge otherwise included in your income is reduced by the amount of that reimbursement. This offers you an advantage where the employer leases the car because you deduct your full lease payment against an amount that is only two-thirds of the lease cost. However, because the reimbursement is taxed punitively to your employer, he or she may be reluctant to permit such an arrangement.

Other Ownership and Operating Expenses

When your employer also pays for such items as insurance, licence, fuel, and repairs and maintenance, you may have an additional taxable benefit. The benefit is equivalent to 13 cents per personal kilometre driven, including 0.65 cents for the GST. This same amount (13 cents per kilometre) may also be used for Quebec tax purposes and includes the GST and the Quebec sales tax. The rate of 13 cents per kilometre is periodically revised.

Election in Respect of Operating Expenses

If you use the car primarily for business, you may elect to include in income in respect of operating expenses paid by your employer an amount equal to one-half of the standby charge. This is an alternative to the amount included based on the calculation at a rate of 13 cents per kilometre mentioned above (10 cents per kilometre for automobile salespeople). Revenue Canada has suggested informally that, for this purpose, "primarily" means more than 50 per cent. If you elect to use this method, you must notify your employer in writing before the end of the applicable year that you are making the election.

Shareholders

The rules for employee automobile benefits generally apply equally to a shareholder of a corporation.

TAX ASPECTS FOR EMPLOYERS AND SELF-EMPLOYED INDIVIDUALS

Allowances

A reasonable allowance paid to an employee for business purposes and based on the number of business kilometres driven in the year is not included in the employee's income. To lessen the administrative difficulty of maintaining mileage records for each employee on a regular basis, Revenue Canada will allow a tax-free fixed allowance to be paid to an employee during the year, provided the following conditions exist:

- There is a pre-established per-kilometre rate.
- The rate and the advance are reasonable.
- At the earlier of the calendar year end or the date the employee ceases to be employed, the actual kilometres travelled for business purposes are calculated. If the employer has overpaid, the employee must refund the excess to the employer. If the employee was underpaid, the employer will make up the difference.
- The employee is not required to include the amount in income under any other provision of the Income Tax Act.

Deductible Expenditures

If your employees use their own cars for business, you may deduct certain allowances or reimbursements you pay them in respect of the business use. In addition, you are eligible for an input tax credit in respect of the GST paid on employee-reimbursed expenditures and the GST deemed to be included in the amount of paid allowances. For QST purposes, you are also eligible for the credit for expenditures on which the QST is paid and the QST deemed to be included in the amount of paid allowances, except for large businesses ($6 million or more of gross income).

If you provide cars to your employees, your deductible amounts generally are limited to non-capital, "reasonable" expenses incurred for the purpose of earning income from a business, profession, or property.

Accordingly, you may deduct all leasing or ownership costs up to the maximum amounts mentioned above, and reasonable operating costs, parking costs, and so forth for the autos provided. You also may deduct interest expense incurred on debt used directly to purchase the autos up to a maximum of $300 ($250 for autos acquired after June 17, 1987, and before September 1, 1989) per month per car, for the period the loans are outstanding.

Employer Deductions in Respect of Employee-Provided Autos

As an employer, you can deduct certain distance-based car allowances paid to an employee in respect of the use of his or her car for the benefit of your business, even when these are not reported as taxable income of the employee. You may deduct fully any car allowances or similar payments that are reported on the employee's T4 as fully taxable.

You will be permitted to deduct tax-free allowances to an employee to the extent that they do not exceed 33 cents for each of the first 5,000 business kilometres driven by the employee in a year, and 27 cents for each additional business kilometre. An additional 4 cents per kilometre is allowed in the Yukon and the Northwest Territories.

You may deduct payments made regarding fuel, maintenance, and repairs in full, although the part of these costs related to personal use of the car will be taxable income to the employee.

Employer Deductions in Respect of Company-Provided Autos

If your company purchases or leases autos that are provided to employees, you will be required to calculate a standby charge, as discussed above, and include the taxable benefit on your employees' T4s (Relevé 1 in Quebec). Although you are required to pay GST and QST (from 1996 for small businesses and from 1998 for large corporations) on the benefit, you may be able to claim the GST and the QST on the purchase price or the lease cost of the car, subject to the maximum amounts prescribed.

Company-Owned Cars

Your company is permitted regular CCA (capital cost allowance) deductions for autos that it owns and that are used in business. Existing CCA rules apply to autos costing the maximum prescribed amount, or less. The autos will be included in the current CCA class 10, which allows a 30 per cent CCA rate. Current recapture, half-year, terminal loss, and pooling rules continue to apply for cars meeting the criteria described above.

If you purchase a car costing in excess of the maximum prescribed cost, each car must be included in a separate CCA class 10.1. The other tax measures for employees described above in the section "Deductions for Owned Vehicles" also apply to employers.

Leased Cars

If the company provides leased autos to its employees, the maximum deduction regarding the lease cost is the same as the deduction available to individuals, as described above. Additional tax rules exist to prevent refundable amounts paid to the lessor from reducing the monthly amount of rent and indirectly increasing the maximum allowable deduction.

You should note that if you provide your employees with leased autos, any reimbursement by an employee of your lease expense will reduce the deductible portion of your cost. This can have a very punitive effect in the case of luxury cars. For instance, if you pay $1,800 per month for a lease entered into on October 1, 1996, your maximum deduction before any reimbursement may be $748 (for an Ontario resident). If the employee reimbursement is $748 or greater, you obtain no deduction. If the reimbursement is less than $748, it must be deducted from the $748 allowable deduction.

PLANNING FOR BUSINESS USE OF AUTOMOBILES

In most cases, specific review of existing policies and available alternatives is necessary to maximize tax deductions and the benefits to employees. In addition, one must consider the ramifications of the Goods and Services Tax.

Such analysis suggests that you should examine different approaches. For instance, perhaps you should

- consider an interest-free loan instead of a car allowance or a company car;
- consider having the employer provide a leased car instead of a purchased car;
- lease the car initially and purchase it at a later date; or
- consider having a car available to you that is used exclusively, or at least 90 per cent, for business.

You should consult your professional advisor to see whether particular approaches can result in significant savings over the costs that might otherwise be incurred.

CHAPTER TEN

Estate Planning

You might be inclined to skip this chapter, in the mistaken belief that you are either not old enough or not rich enough to have an "estate" that is worth planning. The fact is that virtually everyone over the age of majority should give some thought to what will happen to his or her assets in the event of death, and should make arrangements so that financially dependent family members are adequately provided for.

Each year, thousands of Canadians die in accidents, and a large number of them die without having a will. Although the odds are that you will live to a ripe old age, you owe it to yourself, and to your family, to "put your house in order".

Estate planning is the ongoing process of creating and maintaining a program designed to preserve your accumulated wealth and ensure its most effective and beneficial distribution to succeeding generations, according to your wishes.

Several developments in recent years have affected virtually all estate plans and those who are contemplating an estate planning program:

- The abolition on February 22, 1994, of the $100,000 lifetime capital gains exemption can alter the way in which assets are passed on to succeeding generations.

- The constant tightening up of the rules preventing income splitting among family members can necessitate the restructuring of many estate planning approaches.
- The alternative minimum tax (AMT) can affect a number of upper-income Canadians, particularly those with "tax shelter" type investments.
- New or revised family-law acts in several provinces have a great effect on the transfer of assets from one generation to the next.

In addition, on January 1, 1994, the new Civil Code came into effect in Quebec, which contained a number of changes to the chapter on Successions.

OBJECTIVES

In general, the objectives of estate planning are to

- ensure that you and your family are provided for adequately now and in the future (i.e., during your retirement), and that your heirs are adequately provided for after your death;
- distribute assets according to your wishes, both during your lifetime and on your death, while ensuring that the maximum benefits available accrue to your beneficiaries;
- minimize various forms of wealth erosion, taxes being the most prominent, both now and in the future.

Your estate planning objectives should be realistic. More importantly, your estate plan should be reviewed frequently and be flexible enough to accommodate unexpected changes in your financial or personal situation, as well as changes beyond your control, such as new legislative developments.

Financial Considerations

The first step in developing an estate plan is to determine where you stand today in terms of assets, liabilities, and income.

You should also try to project the future direction of your affairs, including possible inheritances, asset liquidations such as sale of a business or property, paying off mortgages, education costs for children, acquiring a recreation or retirement property, and so on. At the same time, you should attempt to assess how the economy's performance might affect your assets and income in the future. Using the "rule of 72", if inflation averages 6 per cent a year, one dollar today will be worth 50 cents in today's dollars in approximately 12 years, and 25 cents in 24 years. If the rate of inflation is 4 per cent, the same result will occur in 18 and 36 years, respectively.

Estate Planning Advisor's Requirements

A professional estate planner needs accurate and up-to-date information concerning your financial affairs, as well as a clear understanding of your financial and personal objectives. He or she must be as well informed about your financial affairs as you are.

An effective estate plan requires the cooperation and input of a number of individuals, including your accountant, lawyer, insurance agent, financial advisor, and to some extent your business associates. It is also recommended that you involve your spouse in setting your estate planning objectives. If your affairs are the least bit complicated and your spouse is expected to manage them on your death, involving him or her now makes good sense. However, this may not suit everyone.

Tax Planning Objectives

From a tax point of view, your estate planning objectives can be summarized as follows:

- Minimize and defer taxes now and in the future, to preserve your accumulated wealth.
- Shift any potential tax burden associated with a particular asset to your heirs so that taxes become payable only when your heirs eventually sell the asset.

- Minimize taxes at death so that as much as possible of your accumulated wealth passes to your heirs.

YOUR CHANGING ESTATE PLAN

To assist you in formulating your own estate planning objectives, the following is a summary of the type of estate planning considerations that a typical family might contemplate throughout the years. However, your own estate plan will depend on the particular circumstances of you and your family.

Estate Planning Early in Life

During the period from your mid-twenties to about age 40, it is likely that you will have a spouse and start a family, will have little in the way of substantial assets, and will be establishing yourself in your career or business. In this case, your goal is to protect your dependants in the event that you or your spouse dies, or becomes otherwise unable to provide for them.

Your estate plan may extend no further than paying down the mortgage on the family home, and ensuring that you have sufficient life insurance (likely term insurance) and long-term disability insurance in place.

It is likely that your will would leave all your assets outright to your spouse.

Once you have more income to devote to estate planning, you will likely want to start saving for future acquisitions, for your children's education, and for your retirement.

You will likely contribute to registered retirement savings plans (RRSPs) for both yourself and your spouse.

At some point, you may find it advantageous to pay higher premiums to obtain the added security and investment benefits available with permanent life insurance.

Planning in Middle Age

From your forties to your mid-fifties, you may well have more substantial assets and be enjoying a larger income. However, you may also be facing increased expenditures such as post-secondary education for your children.

During this period you will continue contributing to a retirement plan, whether an RRSP or a registered pension plan. You may feel you can discontinue your term life insurance policy, while continuing with coverage under a permanent policy.

This may also be a good time to restructure your business affairs and investments to reduce current taxes and facilitate the accumulation of savings and other assets for your retirement.

Planning for Retirement

Once you have reached your mid-fifties, it is time to give serious consideration to planning for your retirement.

You must ensure that you will have sufficient retirement income to cover your needs and savings to cover unforeseen events.

You will likely continue with contributions to your RRSPs or pension plan, and you will probably continue to make additional investments. You might want to determine what type of retirement income will best suit your needs once your RRSPs and pension plans have matured. If you have a business, you may wish to sell it to further supplement your retirement income, or to pass the management of it to others.

It is also time to consider how you wish to dispose of your assets upon your death.

The deemed disposition rules in the Income Tax Act impose a tax on unrealized capital gains at the time of your death, which could seriously erode the value of your assets. However, by careful disposition of your assets during your lifetime and with a carefully drafted will, you may be able to minimize the tax consequences of the deemed disposition rules. You may want to consider gifting some of your assets to your heirs during your lifetime, or establishing trusts for their benefit to take effect either during your lifetime or after your death.

YOUR WILL

In your will, you appoint the executor(s) of your estate, name your beneficiaries, and provide for the distribution of your assets according to your wishes. It is important that you consult your spouse in the preparation of your will so that he or she understands the reasons for the provisions that are included. If your spouse agrees with the terms of the will, he or she will be less likely to use family-law rules to attack the will after your death.

The Executor

The role of the executor, like that of a trustee, under a will involves onerous responsibilities. You should consider not only the willingness of the person to serve, but also his or her appropriateness for the position. Two of the major criteria are the familiarity of the person with your affairs and the technical competence required to manage your affairs.

The executor is charged with interpreting your wishes as expressed in your will and in other documents, and carrying them out to the best of his or her ability.

He or she should be empowered by the provisions of your will to make virtually all decisions concerning your estate that you have not anticipated.

Most importantly, your executor is charged with maintaining the value of your estate until assets are distributed to the beneficiaries. Thus, if he or she feels your business would benefit from outside management help before your beneficiaries take it over, your will must empower him or her to undertake this arrangement. If this is not the case, and your spouse or your children are incapable of managing the business once they gain control, there is little the executor can do but advise them to bring in outside expertise, or perhaps advise them to sell the business before its value seriously declines.

Bear in mind that a great deal of what happens after your death depends on the arrangements you have made before you die. If your instructions are not specific enough, your executor, although acting in good faith, may misinterpret your wishes or may see his or her powers contested in court.

Dying Intestate

In the absence of a will, the distribution of property is decided by provincial law relating to intestate succession and family law.

Such law varies from province to province. For example, the law in several provinces provides that, if a person dies without a will, a reserve must be set aside for the surviving spouse. The spouse receives an amount equal to the reserve and shares the balance with the children, if any. Since this type of distribution is arbitrary, it will not in most circumstances satisfy the wishes of the deceased and the needs of individual family members. In Quebec, if a person dies without a will, one-third of the estate is transferred to the surviving spouse and two-thirds is transferred to the children. It will also be necessary to take into account the family patrimony, the value of which will be divided in equal parts between the spouse and the heirs.

Reviewing Your Will

A good rule of thumb is that your will should be reviewed, and revised if necessary, at least every five years. Your will should be revised immediately in the event of the death of an intended beneficiary or the executor, or because of changes in your family situation or financial circumstances. The coming into force of the new Civil Code is another reason why Quebec residents should have a professional review and, if necessary, modify their will.

Changes in the law may also affect the validity of your will. For instance, in some provinces, legislation respecting division of matrimonial property will override the provisions of your will. This is the case in Quebec with the family patrimony. Furthermore, legislation in most provinces (not including Quebec) provides that you may not totally disinherit your spouse or a dependant. Do not forget to have all the other parts of your estate plan reviewed, such as insurance policies and retirement savings and pension plans. You must remember to change beneficiary designations, or a substantial part of your estate may go to someone you no longer wish to benefit.

To avoid pitfalls and difficulties in the future, professional legal advice should be sought in all cases from lawyers (notaries in Quebec) experienced in wills and family law. It is also advisable to have your tax advisor review the will before you sign it.

TAXATION ON DEATH

If you understand how taxation applies on death, you should be better equipped to decide how to provide effectively for the distribution of your assets in your will, and possibly how to distribute assets during your lifetime.

There are no Canadian death taxes (estate taxes), federal or provincial, levied on the value of the assets that pass to beneficiaries. Only income amounts received (or deemed to be received) by the deceased and capital gains realized (or deemed to be realized) are subject to income tax.

On death, four distinct taxpaying entities may result: the deceased, the estate (as long as it has not been settled by the executor), any ongoing trusts created under the deceased's will, and, finally, the beneficiaries.

Deemed Disposition Rules

In the year of death, an individual's taxation year runs from January 1 to the date of death. A final return of income, the "terminal return", must be filed. All income earned to the date of death must be reported. This includes interest, rents, royalties, annuities, remuneration from employment, and other amounts payable on a periodic basis that were accrued but not due at the time of death, as well as amounts due but not paid. Also included are net taxable capital gains or losses realized prior to death and not included in income in a previous year.

In addition, the deceased is deemed to have disposed of all capital property immediately before death for consideration equal to its fair market value immediately before death. These deemed dispositions can result in capital gains and losses, as well as a terminal loss or recapture of depreciation already claimed, which must be included in the terminal tax return.

Resource properties are defined in the act to be something other than capital property. A deemed disposition of a resource property at death results in the inclusion of the full fair market value as income on the terminal tax return.

A large tax assessment on the "profit" from these deemed dispositions may result. Since there has been no actual sale of assets, the estate may have difficulty paying any taxes that are levied. It should be noted that the alternative minimum tax (AMT) is not applicable in the year of death.

An individual may avoid some of the adverse tax consequences of the deemed disposition rules in two specific situations:

- If property of any kind is transferred to a spouse or spousal trust, no capital gains, recapture of depreciation, etc., arise on death, unless elected otherwise, and the spouse or spousal trust inherits the deceased's tax cost (i.e., the cost at which the deceased acquired or was deemed to have acquired the property). However, before using this method of relieving taxes in respect of property qualifying for the $500,000 lifetime capital gains exemption, it should be ensured that the deceased has fully used this exemption. When a principal residence is transferred to a spouse or spousal trust, the spouse or spousal trust retains the deceased's principal residence exemption.
- If farm property, an interest in a family farm partnership, or shares in a family farm corporation are bequeathed to a child, grandchild, or great-grandchild of the deceased, there is a complete tax deferral on the transfer and the child assumes the deceased's tax cost. An election can be made to not defer the tax either fully or partially, which increases the tax cost of the farm property for the child; however, make sure that the $500,000 lifetime capital gains exemption of the deceased has been fully used up, either before or on death.

These situations are commonly known as "rollovers". Your heirs assume any potential tax liability, which will be payable only when they dispose of or are deemed to dispose of the property.

Optional Tax Returns

If the deceased was the proprietor of, or a partner in, a business, was a beneficiary of a testamentary trust, or had earned "rights or things" (which are generally unrealized income amounts at the date of death), the executor of the estate may have the option of reporting some of the business, trust, or "rights or things" income on three additional separate returns.

The advantage in filing these separate returns is that each return treats the deceased as a separate person.

Full personal tax credits are permitted on each return, which can produce a tax saving, and the splitting of income among the different returns produces a further saving because of the graduated tax rate system.

Taxation of the Estate

Frequently, income-producing assets are held by the estate in trust before passing to specific beneficiaries. Generally, all income earned and received by the estate from the date of death is taxed in the estate, except for income payable or distributed to beneficiaries, or elected to be attributed to a preferred beneficiary, in which cases it is taxed in the hands of the beneficiaries.

Your will should be drafted to empower the executor of your estate to undertake some testamentary tax planning that can reduce taxes in your terminal return and reduce the impact of taxes on your beneficiaries.

Foreign Death Taxes

If you have any assets located in the United States, or if you or any of your beneficiaries is a citizen or resident of the United States, U.S. federal estate tax and state inheritance taxes may apply.

The Third Protocol amending the Canada–U.S. Income Tax Convention came into force in November 1995, and significantly changed the rules on death taxes with respect to U.S. property. In certain circumstances, tax refunds may be claimed for deaths occurring after November 10, 1988. If you own U.S. assets, you should consult with your tax advisor to determine what steps, if any, might be taken to reduce or eliminate the U.S. estate tax exposure.

PLANNING TECHNIQUES

There is often a "cost" involved in implementing some of the estate planning strategies outlined below. A tax saving could be accompanied by loss of control over the related asset, or perhaps the overall flexibility of your estate plan might be impaired to some extent. The tools and techniques that you might use depend on your personal and financial situation and your estate planning objectives.

Gifting

The most direct method of accomplishing the more common estate planning goals is to gift assets to your potential heirs during your lifetime. Since ownership is transferred, the future capital appreciation of the assets and the related future tax liability are also transferred. However, there are three drawbacks to gifting.

First, if the asset is transferred to your spouse or a related child under the age of 18, you will be subject to "attribution rules". In other words, any investment income (that is, interest, dividend, and rental income) earned on the property is taxed in your hands until the marriage breaks down (death, divorce, or separation) or until the year the child turns 18. Also, the capital gain on the sale of such transferred property is attributed to you, except in the case of transfers to minor children. (See Chapter 4.)

Second, since ownership of the asset is transferred, you lose control over the asset and you no longer have access to its future income-earning capability.

Third, when you gift an asset to any person, except your spouse, during your lifetime, you generally are deemed to have received proceeds of disposition equal to the fair market value of the asset at that time, and you must immediately recognize for tax purposes any resulting capital gain or loss.

As in the case of deemed dispositions that occur on death, there are certain exceptions to the above deemed disposition *inter vivos* rule. You may be able to defer the tax via a rollover when

- property is transferred to a spouse or a spousal trust (although future capital gains and losses will be attributed back to you);
- farm property is transferred to a child, grandchild, or great-grandchild.

If you are a shareholder of a Canadian private corporation that uses all or substantially all of the fair market value of its assets in carrying on an active business primarily in Canada, or own qualified farm property, you may be eligible for the $500,000 lifetime capital gains exemption on the disposition of shares of the company. (See Chapter 7.) This exemption may be limited to $400,000 if you have already taken full advantage of the $100,000 cumulative exemption for capital gains realized or deemed to have been realized on other property.

If you have not already used up your $500,000 exemption, you may want to gift enough of your shares in the company to your children to trigger a $500,000 capital gain and thereby utilize the exemption. However, this strategy may not make sense if you are planning to sell the company to outsiders. It might be better to save the exemption for the arm's-length sale, rather than use it for a "paper transaction" between family members, keeping in mind, however, that this exemption could also be abolished.

Income Splitting

The prime objective of income splitting is to have income that normally would be taxed in your hands at a high tax rate instead taxed in the hands of a relative, usually your spouse or child, at a lower tax rate. A detailed examination of income splitting and its effects is contained in Chapter 4.

The Use of Trusts

In its simplest form, a trust merely involves the holding of property by one person for the benefit of another person. In more technical terms, a trust is created when a settlor transfers property to a trustee, who holds the property for the benefit of a beneficiary. A trust may be either testamentary (i.e., arising upon your death) or *inter vivos* (i.e., arising during your lifetime).

A trust can be a useful and flexible device in that it allows you to transfer ownership of an asset to an intended heir, while you, or actually the trustee of the trust, are able to maintain control over the asset.

It permits you to accomplish a number of your estate planning goals. Trusts may be used for such varied purposes as funding a child's education, providing for handicapped children, or obtaining professional property management.

To achieve a tax saving, you must first relinquish ownership of the assets held by the trust, although in some cases you may still control the management and operation of the trust itself, and, second, you must avoid the attribution rules. See Chapter 4.

An *inter vivos* trust is generally subject to the same rules as individuals and is taxed at the top personal rate. Testamentary trusts are taxed more favourably at the progressive tax rates applied to individuals.

However, if trust income is distributed to a beneficiary, whether directly by means of an actual distribution, or by means of the preferred beneficiary election (see below), or is distributable, such amounts are deducted from trust income and taxed in the hands of the beneficiary, assuming the attribution rules do not apply. This can result in some tax savings if the beneficiary is taxed at a lower marginal rate.

The Income Tax Act provides that certain forms of income earned in a trust retain their character when distributed to beneficiaries and taxed in their hands. For example, eligible

Canadian taxable dividends received by a trust and distributed to a beneficiary make the beneficiary eligible for the dividend tax credit.

Preferred Beneficiary Election. By making this election, income earned by the trust is taxed in the hands of the beneficiary, even though the income remains in the trust. Beginning in 1996, this election is available only to beneficiaries entitled to the mental or physical impairment tax credit. A preferred beneficiary must be a Canadian resident and one of the following:

- the settlor of the trust, or his or her spouse or former spouse;
- a child, grandchild, or great-grandchild of the settlor;
- the spouse (but not former spouse) of a child, grandchild, or great-grandchild of the settlor.

In addition, the settlor must contribute more to the trust than any other taxpayer.

Deemed Disposition Rule for Trusts. Special rules prevent trusts from holding property for an indefinite period, thereby deferring the inclusion of capital gains in income for tax purposes. The general rule provides for a deemed disposition by a trust of all its capital property every 21 years for notional proceeds of sale equal to the fair market value of the property. However, the general rule does not apply to a trust with an exempt beneficiary living on the day the 21-year rule should normally apply, if a choice has been made to that effect. The spouse and children of the individual who has disposed of the property in favour of the trust may be deemed exempt beneficiaries, but not the grandchildren. This exception to the general rule is supposed to be abolished as of January 1, 1999.

Estate Freezing

An estate freeze is a method of organizing your affairs to permit any future appreciation in the value of selected assets to accrue to others, usually your children.

An estate freeze is not a gift. If assets are gifted to a child, no value is received in return and control is lost. Under an estate freeze, you retain, or at least have access to, the current value of the frozen assets; only the future increases in value are transferred to the child. It is also possible for you to retain control over those assets. Unlike estate freezing, gifting assets to your child eliminates tax on your death, but it also may result in an immediate tax liability and probably achieves none of your other estate planning goals.

Direct Sale. Selling an asset to your child, the simplest of estate freezes, may achieve some or even all the goals. Tax is eliminated on death, but you must include any capital gain in income for tax purposes in the year of sale. Normally, you would take back a note payable from the child as payment of the sale price. Thus you can dispose of a growth asset and obtain a fixed-value asset in its place. Interest may not be payable on the note; however, if this is the case, the attribution rules will apply. It is also questionable whether you can legally sell an asset to a minor.

You can claim a reserve (i.e., not recognize the full capital gain) if you have not received all proceeds from the sale and the unpaid proceeds are not yet due. The taxable capital gain must be brought into your income over, at most, the succeeding four or nine years, depending on the type of asset sold. When the reserve amount is included in income, it is eligible for the $500,000 lifetime capital gains exemption, provided the related eligible property was disposed of after 1984.

The fact that you are able to demand partial or full payment on the note at any time may or may not represent some form of control over the asset. Transferring the asset to a trust of which the child is a beneficiary may permit you to exercise more control over the asset.

Corporate Freeze. Most individuals are concerned with freezing assets that are likely to increase substantially in value in the future. The most common are business assets, usually in the form of shares of a private corporation controlled by the individual. Using a corporation in an estate freeze provides the individual with considerable flexibility and, if properly structured, enables him or her to achieve each of the estate freezing goals mentioned above.

Taking Advantage of Tax Provisions

Principal Residence Exemption. Detailed rules on the principal residence exemption are contained in Chapter 2. A number of estate planning options involve changes in the ownership of a principal residence.

If two residences are currently owned by a married couple (e.g., a city home and a summer cottage), consideration might be given to transferring ownership of one property, say, the cottage, to children or grandchildren who reside in the residence for at least part of the year. This may involve a slight cost currently, i.e., tax on the capital gain from the property appreciating since 1981. Any future gain realized on the disposition of the other property retained by the couple would generally be tax-free under the principal residence rules. As well, since the attribution rules do not apply to capital gains realized on property that was transferred to children, whether or not they are under 18, any capital gain realized when the cottage is subsequently sold would be taxable in the hands of the children. Alternatively, the cottage could be designated as the principal residence of a child or children over 18 or married, and thus they would benefit from the full exemption.

Of course, if you sell or gift the cottage directly to the children, you and your spouse no longer have any legal right to occupy it. Taking back a demand note payable on the sale may give you some control over the property, but perhaps not enough to suit your wishes. One solution might be to give the property to a discretionary trust for you and your children. The trust agreement might be structured to permit you to give the cottage to a particular child at some time in the future, while ensuring that the future increase in value accrues to the ultimate owner.

Registered Retirement Savings Plans. RRSPs are probably the most common tax deferral vehicles in use today. Stated simply, the immediate tax benefit of an RRSP is that it reduces annual income for tax purposes (within specified limits) by the amount of the annual contribution and shelters the income accumulating in the plan from taxation. As well, an RRSP will provide you with a fund that, on your death, might be passed on to your spouse, who is subject to a lower tax rate, and, in certain circumstances, to your children. Contributions to your registered pension plan also have the immediate tax benefit of reducing your taxable income. (See Chapter 6.)

Spouse and Spousal Trust Rollovers. If you bequeath capital property directly to your spouse or a qualifying spousal trust, the property can be rolled over (i.e., transferred) at your tax cost with no resulting taxation at the time of your death. For these spousal rollover rules to apply, certain criteria must be met:

- You must have been resident in Canada immediately before death.
- The ownership of the property must actually be transferred to your spouse or a qualifying spousal trust.
- If the transfer is to your spouse, he or she must have been resident in Canada immediately prior to your death.
- The spousal trust must be testamentary (i.e., one created by your will) and must reside in Canada when the property vests in the trust.
- Vesting in the spouse or spousal trust generally must occur within 36 months of your death.
- If the property is transferred to a spousal trust, your spouse must be entitled to receive all the income during his or her lifetime and no other person may receive or have the use of any income or capital during that period.

A certain amount of planning can be undertaken after your death by your estate's executor. For example, he or she may elect that the rollover provisions not apply to selected assets. This may allow the full use of your losses carried forward and, if the election is made in respect of qualified property, your $500,000 capital gains exemption, both of which will reduce the future tax liability of your spouse.

Spousal Rollover of Reserves. With one exception, no reserves can be claimed in the terminal income tax return. The full amount of any reserve outstanding is added to income in the year of death. The one exception occurs where a qualifying spouse, or spousal trust, inherits the rights to receive an amount that gave rise to the deduction of the reserve. Providing the deceased was resident in Canada immediately before death and the executor of the estate and the spouse or spousal trust jointly elect, a deduction for such reserves can be claimed in the terminal return of the deceased. The reserve then flows through to the spouse, or spousal trust, who ultimately pays tax on the income deferred.

The amount of the allowable reserve and the length of time from the date of sale within which the income or capital gain must be included in income depend on the type of property that was disposed. Capital gains must be included in income over five years, while income from property sold in the ordinary course of business may be recognized over a maximum of four years. Capital gains arising from the transfer of farm assets and shares of eligible small business corporations to a child may be spread over ten years.

Life Insurance

Life insurance plays an important role in estate planning. It can be used for a variety of purposes:

- to provide a base for generating investment income to replace earnings;

- as a tax-sheltered investment vehicle, if properly structured, for the accumulation of funds during your lifetime, with a tax-free payout on your death;
- to help the surviving shareholder of a closely held corporation finance the purchase of shares from the estate or heirs of a deceased shareholder;
- to provide liquidity on death to cover the payment of income taxes and other debts and expenses;
- to provide additional assets to bequeath to a child or children who is/are not involved in a family business. In the absence of the insurance funds, the non-involved children might receive shares of the family business and be in a position to create problems for those running the business.

Insurance proceeds that are payable as a result of the death of the insured are not subject to income tax in the hands of the beneficiary.

Your financial situation and the future needs of your family will dictate the type and quantity of life insurance you should have. While your insurance agent can provide you with details of a wide variety of individual policies available, you might bear in mind that there are two basic types of life insurance: term policies and permanent policies.

The term policy is generally less expensive at a younger age but has a number of disadvantages. For example, you receive no benefits if the policy is cancelled either by the insurer or yourself. There is usually no obligation for an insurer to continue coverage and the policy will likely not be renewed beyond a certain age. Of course, insurance companies now offer many variations on the term policy that have additional features, such as options that guarantee your insurability to almost any age.

While a permanent policy (often referred to as a "whole life" or "universal" policy) initially involves higher premiums, it has the advantage of also serving as an investment vehicle for you. For example, you may usually borrow against your insurance savings at a favourable rate, and you may receive a lump sum if you decide to cash in the policy at a future date. Most permanent policies are structured so that accruing income is not taxed annually; however, borrowing against the cash surrender value or "cashing in" the policy could result in tax.

Insurance arrangements involving the purchase of a deceased shareholder's shares by the surviving shareholders are more complex and require careful planning.

SUCCESSION AND ESTATE PLANNING FOR BUSINESS ASSETS

If you have an interest in a business, it is likely your largest source of income and you may be expecting the business to provide you with a retirement income. You may also foresee eventually passing control of it to your children. On the other hand, you may wish to sell the business to a partner or third party on your retirement, or arrange for professional management while ownership remains with your family. Whatever your goals, you should know a number of planning techniques that can result in substantial tax savings for you and your family.

Most financial planning, including tax and succession planning, is facilitated if the business is incorporated. If your business is not incorporated, but can be, you should discuss the situation with your professional advisor.

Before examining the planning techniques best suited to you, there are a number of considerations you should address. These include the ability of your spouse or children to manage the business, their relative participation in control and ownership, the time frame for transfer of control, the role of key employees, and your own financial needs after retirement.

The remainder of this chapter examines three major succession and estate planning techniques that focus on business assets:

- exemption of the tax on capital gains on the transfer of shares of an eligible small business corporation and deferral and/or exemption of tax on capital gains on the transfer of eligible farm property to your children;
- methods of corporate estate freezing so that the tax consequences of all or part of future growth in the business are passed to your heirs;
- the use of insurance to fund certain succession planning transactions.

Exemption of Tax on Capital Gains on Shares of Small Business Corporations

The deemed disposition rules consider shares to be disposed of for proceeds equal to fair market value immediately before death. As well, on the gifting of the shares to anyone other than your spouse, you are deemed to receive proceeds of disposition equal to the fair market value of the shares.

If the value of the business has increased significantly over the years, a large capital gain will generally result. Such a gain is eligible for the lifetime capital gains exemption. There is an aggregate capital gains exemption of $500,000 which includes the normal $100,000 exemption abolished on February 22, 1994. This exemption applies to gains realized on the disposition of "qualified farm property" or "qualified small business corporation shares". These are defined terms, but if your business is an active business carried on primarily in Canada, and at least 90 per cent of the fair market value of assets of the corporation are used in the business, chances are that it would qualify for the $500,000 capital gains exemption. If your spouse owns part of the small business corporation, he or she also has a $500,000 exemption, which means that tax on up to $1,000,000 of capital gains may be eliminated. If the gain is realized in one particular year, however, you may effectively be subject to the alternative minimum tax (AMT) on the "untaxed" part of the gain.

Rollover of Farming Property

To encourage the children of farmers to continue to operate the family farm after their parents' retirement or death, special rules permit farming assets to be passed from one generation to the next without incurring a tax cost. Similar rollover rules also apply to the transfer of shares of a family farm corporation (or a holding corporation that owns such shares) and to the transfer of an interest in a family farm partnership. Also, the $500,000 capital gains exemption is available for gains realized on the disposition of qualified farm property, to the extent it has not been used to shelter gains from the disposition of qualified small business corporation shares.

Rollover provisions merely postpone the taxation of a gain; they do not reduce it. However, transferring the property under the lifetime exemption will increase the child's tax cost of the property, resulting in a smaller capital gain whenever the child disposes of the property. The child may utilize the $500,000 lifetime exemption when the property is sold, provided the exemption still exists at that time.

Estate Freezing Techniques

After deciding on the objectives that best suit your estate planning needs, particular techniques must be chosen that will achieve your intended objectives with the optimum tax advantage. The techniques briefly discussed below all involve "freezing" the present value of your business so that all or part of the future growth and the resulting tax consequences are deferred to your heirs. However, these techniques may be used to freeze the value of almost any assets having inherent taxable capital gains.

An estate freeze is generally undertaken when assets are likely to increase substantially in value over the long term. The goals of the freeze are usually to eliminate or defer, if possible, immediate tax in your hands, to ensure that future growth of the asset will benefit your children, and to allow you to maintain control of the asset.

The choice of technique used to freeze the assets will depend upon a number of considerations, including the

- nature of the assets to be frozen;
- size of the estate;
- extent of control you wish to exercise over the frozen assets;
- number of parties to be involved in the freeze;
- immediate tax cost, if any, that might result from the freeze, bearing in mind access by you and your spouse to the $500,000 lifetime capital gains exemption on qualified property;
- degree of complexity that you can tolerate;
- professional fees that will be incurred;
- degree of flexibility and reversibility desired.

The following discussion assumes that your active business assets are owned by a corporation controlled by you. The corporate structure generally facilitates effective succession and estate planning. If business assets are not held by such a corporation, it is usually a relatively simple matter to arrange.

Direct Sale. Perhaps the simplest method of freezing your interest in shares of a privately held company is to sell the shares directly to your adult children. The sale would take place at fair market value, and you would take back a promissory note for the balance of the sale price not received in cash. There should be an agreement of purchase and sale that sets out the details of the sale, such as terms of payment, the due date of any unpaid amount, and whether the unpaid balance is subject to interest. It is not necessary to charge interest on the unpaid balance owed by your children, but the attribution rules will then apply.

There are some disadvantages to a direct sale. You will be taxed on any capital gain realized in excess of any gain eligible for your $500,000 lifetime capital gains exemption. You also may become subject to the alternative minimum tax. However, you may claim a reserve (i.e., exclude from income) on a portion of the taxable gain if you do not immediately receive all proceeds of disposition. When amounts claimed under the reserve provisions are eventually brought back into income for tax purposes, they will be eligible for your $500,000 lifetime capital gains exemption. Remember that, even if you gift the shares to your children, you will be deemed to receive proceeds of disposition equal to their fair market value.

A second disadvantage of a direct sale is that you could lose control of the business, assuming sufficient voting shares are sold to your children. This may be overcome if you subscribe for new voting preferred shares that carry more votes than the existing common shares. Alternatively, you may be able to exercise some control by placing the common shares in escrow (i.e., maintaining possession and control of them) until the demand note has been entirely paid off.

Another disadvantage of a direct sale is that, unless cash is paid for the shares, the amount owing to you remains with the corporation and may therefore continue to be at risk. A solution might be to have your children take out a loan to pay you for the shares, rather than accepting a demand note from them; however, this would necessitate recognizing the entire capital gain almost immediately for tax purposes, and risks triggering the alternative minimum tax. As an alternative, the consideration could be part cash (from the outside loan) and part note (from the children).

Sale to a Holding Company. A common method of freezing the value of shares in an existing company involves the use of a new holding company specifically set up to acquire such shares. The children involved in the freeze would incorporate a company and acquire all its common shares for a nominal amount. You would transfer your shares in the operating company to the newly incorporated holding company, which generally can be done on a tax-deferred basis. You would take back voting preferred shares (with a value equal to the shares transferred into the holding company) in the new company as consideration for the transfer.

Over the last few years, changes in family law in certain provinces, in which assets acquired by a couple during their marriage are divided equally on dissolution of the marriage, could result in a significant portion of a parent's assets being transferred to the former spouse of a child. In order to circumvent this possibility, in the above scenario the parent would acquire all the common shares of the holding company as well as the preferred shares. The parent would then gift the common shares to his or her child(ren). This would exclude the common shares from the matrimonial property of the married child in most instances, since assets inherited or received by way of gift are excluded from the matrimonial property. In Quebec, shares of a private or public company are not included in the matrimonial property.

Any future appreciation in the value from the operation of the business now accrues to your children. You could retain control of the operating company by means of voting preferred shares in the holding company. This permits you to set dividends and a reasonable salary according to your income requirements and allows you to run the business much as you did before.

One disadvantage of the use of a holding company in an estate freeze is that a capital gain or deemed dividend may arise on the redemption or disposition of the preferred shares (that you acquired as consideration for the transfer of your shares) during your lifetime. However, all or a portion of the capital gain could be exempt under your $500,000 lifetime capital gains exemption if the shares were considered as qualified property at the time of redemption or disposal. As well, it might be necessary to obtain a professional valuation of your shares.

Asset Freeze. As an alternative to transferring the shares of an operating company to a holding company, you may wish to consider freezing the value of these shares by selling the underlying operating assets to a new company incorporated by your children. This method of estate freezing may involve considerable work and expense, and sales or other transfer taxes could result. However, in some situations an asset freeze is the best approach. For example, you may own a multifaceted business that you want to break up into separate corporations, each to be owned by one child.

Internal Freeze. It may be possible to reorganize the existing share capital structure of your company to accomplish an estate freeze. Where the applicable provincial or federal companies law permits, you may exchange all your existing common shares for voting preferred shares of a certain type. Subsequent to this transaction, a new class of common shares is created that the children purchase at a nominal amount. The result of such a reorganization is that you freeze the current value of your holdings in the operating company, and your children participate in the future growth in value of the company through their ownership of the common shares. This type of freeze is relatively simple, does not require a new corporate entity, and provides you with preferred shares that should give you a fixed income, if desired. Of course, as with other freezes where no cash is received, there is always the problem that the money owed to you is tied up in the corporation and therefore exposed to some risk.

Choosing the Best Freeze Vehicle. The choice of freeze vehicle you ultimately make should not be based solely on income tax considerations. For example, a partial estate freeze should provide better protection from future inflation than a complete freeze. In all cases, it is advisable for you to consult your professional advisors before making a final decision and proceeding to put the plan into action. An estate freeze requires careful planning, not only because of the tax consequences involved, but because it may well be very difficult to thaw (i.e., unwind) the freeze once it has been effected.

Sales to Third Parties

If you own a business, you may want to transfer it to unrelated parties, such as fellow shareholders, partners, or key employees, rather than to your children or spouse. For one thing, your spouse or children may not be able or willing to run the business. Moreover, the partners or other shareholders may not want the children involved.

Arranging a sale to employees may bind your best employees to the business, relieve you of some management headaches as you get older, and assist in an orderly transfer of ownership. A sale could be coupled with a long-term employment contract should you wish to remain involved in the company.

Insurance and Buy–Sell Agreements

Insurance arrangements for business purposes are complex and require careful planning. The purpose of business insurance in the context of estate planning usually is to ensure that there are sufficient funds on hand at your death to enable the business to be dealt with in accordance with your wishes.

Depending on your estate plan, you may want to ensure that your estate will have sufficient liquid assets on hand to pay tax on any taxable capital gains realized on your death. Furthermore, you may want your partner or another shareholder in the corporation to purchase your share of the business on your death.

Buy–Sell Agreement. A buy–sell agreement is basically a contract between business partners or shareholders of a corporation. It is frequently used in estate planning to ensure, for instance, that surviving shareholders have the right or obligation to purchase the shares of a deceased shareholder. It is advantageous both for the surviving shareholders, who may not want a stranger to buy into the corporation, and the family of the deceased, who might otherwise have difficulty selling the shares.

The spousal rollover rules are not applicable to shares that are subject to a compulsory buy–sell agreement, and tax would be paid by the deceased shareholder in the terminal tax return on any resulting capital gain if the $500,000 lifetime capital gains exemption cannot be fully used. However, if the buy–sell agreement is structured in such a way that the surviving shareholder has an option to buy, and the surviving spouse has an option to sell, the shares can first pass to the spouse on a rollover basis. Any capital gain arising on the subsequent sale of the shares by the spouse would be recognized in his or her hands and be eligible for the spouse's own $500,000 lifetime capital gains exemption, if still available, and provided the shares are qualified shares at the time.

Whichever buy–sell method is employed, one thing remains certain—unless there is some method of funding the transaction, the agreement may not be consummated. It is common for life insurance to be used as a means to provide the funds necessary to finance the sale. There are three common methods of employing life insurance as the funding mechanism for a buy–sell agreement.

Criss-Cross Insurance. This is an insurance arrangement where each shareholder of a corporation acquires a life insurance policy on the life of each other shareholder. On the death of one shareholder, the survivors receive the tax-free proceeds of the policy and use the funds to purchase the deceased's shares from his or her estate or beneficiaries. One disadvantage of this method is that the cost of the insurance to each shareholder can vary widely, depending on the ages and health of the other shareholders.

Corporate-Owned Insurance. With this type of policy the corporation insures the lives of its shareholders and receives the proceeds on their deaths. The advantage of this method is that the corporation pays all the insurance premiums and the cost to the shareholders is shared in proportion to their shareholdings. The proceeds are used by the corporation to purchase the deceased's shares, either from the deceased's estate or from the surviving spouse. Generally, neither the deceased nor the spouse will be subject to tax on the buy-back if the arrangement is properly structured. However, the surviving shareholders do not have the cost base of their shares increased on the redemption, which in effect means the deceased's shareholder's gain has been transferred to them. This situation could be compensated for by reducing the redemption price so that more cash is retained in the corporation or by increasing the amount of the insurance.

Pending changes to legislation could make this kind of arrangement less attractive because the deceased would be subject to tax. The changes are complex; however, transitional rules offer protection in certain circumstances. Existing succession plans should be reviewed to see if they qualify for the protection, while business reorganizations should be structured to alleviate the impact of the new rules. Obtaining professional advice is strongly recommended.

Split-Dollar Insurance. Split-dollar insurance is a combination of both criss-cross and corporate-owned insurance. Each shareholder purchases a whole-life type of policy on the other and assigns the cash value of the policy to the company. On the death of a shareholder, the company receives the cash value of the policy, whereas the surviving shareholders receive the face value less the cash value, and use these proceeds to purchase the shares. The advantage of this method is that the company pays most of the premiums.

The use of buy–sell agreements, combined with life insurance funding, should be an integral part of any estate plan where shares of private companies are owned and there are two or more shareholders dealing with each other at arm's length and also in some non-arm's-length situations. In all cases, the insuring method employed should not be chosen without the assistance of a professional advisor.

BEGINNING THE PROCESS

Estate planning is not a once-and-for-all activity. You should view it as an ongoing process, involving a variety of techniques over the years, to suit your changing circumstances. This chapter has focused on the tax aspects of estate planning. There are other factors for you to consider that are of equal or greater importance. Above all, don't rush into a tax-motivated estate plan without giving full consideration to your personal and financial circumstances. Keep in mind that few things in life turn out exactly as we plan them. Your estate plan must have sufficient flexibility built into it so that you can adapt it to fit unforeseen future events.

CHAPTER ELEVEN

Special Tax Measures for Quebec Residents

In general, the Quebec government harmonizes its tax legislation with that of the federal government. On the other hand, there are some differences, especially as regards personal income tax credits. Details of these credit amounts and a few other features particular to the Quebec system are outlined in Chapter 13.

In addition, the Quebec government has tax benefits available to its residents that are offered concurrently by the federal government or are uniquely adapted to the economic needs of the province. They are designed to promote investments in strategic sectors of industry such as mining exploration, film production, and scientific research.

This chapter discusses certain specific tax measures that apply to Quebec residents.

Deductions, Tax Credits, Refunds, and Reductions

Employment Income. Some annual dues are deductible only in Quebec. Of note are annual dues to an association of employees recognized by the Minister whose main objective is the study, safeguarding, and promotion of the economic interests of its members, and also payments required for membership in a professional association or an artistic association recognized by the Minister.

However, beginning in 1997, Quebec will provide a tax credit for union and professional dues, instead of a deduction.

Also, when employment duties are performed outside Canada in certain types of businesses (construction, engineering, etc.), federal legislation provides a tax credit, while Quebec legislation provides for a deduction in calculating taxable income. In both cases, certain conditions must be met in order to have access to these tax benefits.

Tuition Fees. Tuition fees are also treated differently in Quebec. When fees exceed $100, a tax credit equal to 17 per cent is allowed under the federal system. Where the credit is not fully claimed, it may be transferred to a spouse or parent to a maximum of $850.

Under Quebec legislation, tuition fees must be deducted when computing net income and can be claimed only by the student. Moreover, examination fees charged by professional corporations mentioned in Schedule 1 of the Professional Code, i.e., exclusive professions and professions with reserved titles, are deductible when the examinations are required to become a member of one of the corporations or to practise one of the professions mentioned in the schedule.

Child Care Expense. Contrary to the federal legislation, which allows individuals to deduct child care expenses, the Quebec legislation provides a refundable tax credit for these expenses.

Most of the rules in both pieces of legislation are similar when it comes to determining eligible child care expenses. However, there are some differences regarding the maximum eligible amount and the fact that either spouse is allowed to take into account these expenses in his or her income tax return.

Charitable Gifts. A taxpayer making a charitable gift is entitled to a tax credit, just as in the federal system, but the tax credit is different. Under federal legislation, the first $200 of a donation is credited at 17 per cent and the remainder at 29 per cent. Quebec legislation provides a 20 per cent credit on the entire amount donated. Under the federal system, the total amount of gifts that can be deducted is limited to 50 per cent of net income, while it is limited to 20 per cent under the Quebec system. Since May 10, 1995, if the gift is a work of art, the tax credit is generally limited to the selling price of the work of art by the organization to which the gift is given. Moreover, the sale must take place before the end of the fifth calendar year following the year of the gift, failing which, the tax benefit will be forfeited.

Other Items. Some items contained in the Quebec legislation do not have a federal equivalent.

For instance, a person who resides in Quebec on December 31 may be entitled to a real estate tax refund. This credit is available to tenants and homeowners. The size of the credit depends on the individual's total income and that of the spouse, if applicable. It also depends on the aggregate of real estate taxes for the year. For 1996, the maximum credit has been set at $514.

Finally, low- and middle-income families are entitled to a tax reduction. It provides a reduction of income tax, but is not refundable. The amount of the reduction depends on the individual's total income, that of the spouse, and that of any dependent children (if applicable). For 1996, the maximum has been set at $970 per person or $1,500 for a couple with at least one dependent child. Single parents who do not share an independent dwelling with another adult are entitled to a tax reduction of $1,195.

Quebec Stock Savings Plan

In 1979, the Quebec government introduced the stock savings plan (QSSP) to promote stock investments in Quebec companies and reduce the tax burden on individuals residing in the province. Although the QSSP has undergone several adjustments over the years, which have made it much less attractive, it nevertheless remains an interesting method of tax planning if you are prepared to acquire shares on the stock market. It is wise to keep in mind, however, that any tax benefit achieved with a QSSP may decline with the market value of the shares. Consequently, even when shares qualify under the QSSP, the first criterion you should investigate before purchasing shares is still their potential yield and growth. To reduce the risk associated with this type of investment, you can invest through a stock savings plan investment group or investment fund. One of the advantages of these alternative forms of investment is that you will have a share in a more diversified stock portfolio without having to make a considerable investment.

Tax Benefit. If you are a Quebec resident at the close of the tax year and have acquired qualifying shares in a stock savings plan during the year, you may deduct the adjusted cost of these shares from your taxable income, to a maximum of 10 per cent of your total income. Your "total income" is the net income amount that appears on your provincial income tax return, less the capital gains exemption used during the year. Shares must have been acquired prior to the end of the tax year and be included in the stock savings plan before February 1 of the following year to be considered qualifying shares. The allowable deduction is restricted to the "adjusted cost" of your shares; that is, to the full cost of the shares, excluding the cost of borrowing, brokers' commissions, or safekeeping fees. These shares must be issued by "growth corporations", which means corporations with assets of between $2 million and $250 million. Moreover, growth corporations can issue unsecured debentures or preferred shares that entitle the holders to a 50 per cent QSSP deduction. To meet the eligibility requirements, these securities must, in particular, be convertible at any time into common shares carrying voting rights under all circumstances, and they must be listed on the Montreal Exchange.

For example, you purchase shares of growth corporations

for $3,000. In 1996, your net income is $50,000, and you realized a taxable capital gain of $10,000 on the sale of qualified small business corporation shares for which the capital gains exemption has been used. Your QSSP deduction will amount to the lesser of the following:

• Adjusted cost of shares $3,000 × 100%	$ 3,000
• 10% of your total income 10% × ($50,000 – $10,000)	$ 4,000

Your deduction will therefore be $3,000.

Management fees for a QSSP and the cost of borrowing to purchase shares constitute financial expenses and are deductible annually.

Additional Deductions. Shares included in a QSSP entitle the holder to an additional 25 per cent deduction on the cost of the shares when they are acquired under an employee stock option plan. An employer may create a plan to encourage employees to acquire the shares issued by the employer corporation when it goes public. The plan must be available to all employees and executives with more than three months of service and who own less than 5 per cent of the capital stock of the corporation immediately prior to acquiring shares in the stock option plan.

Recovery of Deductions. At the end of the two subsequent calendar years, your stock portfolio must contain shares that have an adjusted cost equal to the amount for which you obtained a deduction. Should this not be the case, you will either have to include a portion or all of the deductions previously allowed in your income for the year in which this condition is not met or reduce the amount of the deduction that you could otherwise claim during the year.

If, for example, in 1994 you acquired $1,000 of shares,

which at the time entitled you to a deduction of 50 per cent, and you sell these shares in 1996, you must, before the end of 1996, acquire replacement shares with an adjusted cost of $500 so that the deduction you obtained will not be added to your income during 1996. You cannot, however, benefit from a new QSSP deduction for the replacement shares.

In addition to newly issued shares, replacement shares also include the shares of growth corporations that already entitle the holder to the QSSP deduction if they are purchased on the secondary market and listed by the Commission des valeurs mobilières du Québec.

Capital Gains and Dividends. Dividends received on shares in stock savings plans are treated as any other dividend received on shares. When the shares are sold, the capital gain or loss is calculated in the usual manner. The tax benefit received does not reduce the actual cost of the shares.

QSSPs versus RRSPs. Unlike the RRSP, which allows only for income tax payments to be deferred, the QSSP offers a real tax saving. The RRSP does, however, reduce your immediate income tax at both the federal and the provincial levels, while the QSSP deduction can be used only in Quebec.

A share in a QSSP cannot be included under another tax plan at the same time. However, you can contribute successively to your QSSP and RRSP using the same funds and, because the deadlines for contributions are different, obtain the QSSP and the RRSP deduction for the same year.

Whereas shares included in a QSSP must be acquired before year end, it is possible to contribute to an RRSP during the first 60 days of the subsequent year. As a result, QSSP shares can be sold at the beginning of the year following the year of acquisition and the sale proceeds used to make a contribution to an

RRSP. To avoid the recovery of deductions, QSSP shares must be replaced before the end of the year in which they are sold, unless the adjusted cost of shares for over two years in your QSSP portfolio allows you to escape this rule. The double deduction is therefore only temporary, but may prove useful if you do not have sufficient liquid assets available at this time of the year.

Cooperative Investment Plan

To encourage investments in certain Quebec cooperatives, the provincial government has introduced the Quebec Cooperative Investment Plan, which provides a deduction to an individual who acquires eligible securities issued by a qualified cooperative. This deduction applies only to a member or worker of the cooperative and to an employee of a partnership to which the qualified cooperative contributes more than 50 per cent of the income.

The deduction and the two-year holding period are calculated in the same manner as under the QSSP. The deduction is equal to 100 per cent of the cost of the securities purchased, not exceeding 10 per cent of total income. The basic deduction is 125 per cent for units issued by small and medium-sized cooperatives, i.e., those with assets of less than $25 million or equity of no more than $10 million.

When a cooperative sets up a "stock ownership plan" (i.e., a plan allowing employees and officers to acquire securities in their cooperative) similar to the one discussed above in the section "Quebec Stock Savings Plan", individuals who acquire such securities are entitled to an additional deduction of 25 per cent, for a total deduction of 125 or 150 per cent of the cost of the shares.

Quebec Business Investment Companies

A Quebec Business Investment Company (QBIC) is a business incorporated in Quebec whose primary activity is to acquire shares of other unrelated eligible private corporations operating mainly in a specific sector such as manufacturing, tourism, export, or environmental protection in Quebec. QBICs are an intermediate financing vehicle between eligible private corporations and investors. QBICs are not listed on the stock market.

Tax Benefit. If you are a Quebec resident on December 31 of a tax year and purchase common shares of a QBIC, you will be entitled to deduct 125 per cent of your purchase price from your taxable income for Quebec income tax purposes, provided it corresponds to your financial commitment. However, this deduction can be taken only when the QBIC invests the money to acquire common shares of an eligible corporation. An additional 25 per cent deduction may be allowed in accordance with the investments the QBIC will make in small or medium-sized businesses located outside main urban centres. Moreover, if the QBIC shares are acquired as part of an employee stock option plan under which employees are encouraged to purchase shares of the employer corporation through a QBIC, another 25 per cent deduction will be granted. Thus, the total deduction could reach 175 per cent.

However, the deduction used in a given year must not exceed 30 per cent of your total income; any portion not claimed in a year due to this limit may be deferred to the five subsequent years.

Investments in a QBIC do not affect contribution limits to RRSPs and QSSPs. Unlike a QSSP, you are not required to keep your securities for at least two years. This is the responsibility of the QBIC. If a QBIC constitutes an "active business" and the other criteria prescribed by law are met, you can even benefit from the $500,000 capital gains exemption on the sale or disposal of these shares.

Certified Quebec Films

The Quebec legislation contains a special mechanism to make it easier for film production companies that are large enough to be listed on the Montreal Exchange to raise outside funds and to enable public corporations to forgo their film and television production tax credit in favour of their shareholders.

It is, therefore, possible to include eligible manpower expenditures, for which such a corporation has forgone the tax credit, in an account, relating to the financing of certified Quebec films, to which an additional deduction of 100 per cent applies.

The last provincial budget has abolished this mechanism for investments made after May 9, 1996.

Mineral Exploration and Oil and Gas Sectors

The acquisition of flow-through shares, whether directly or through a limited partnership, enables the holder to benefit from tax breaks for Quebec income tax purposes. Additional deductions are also allowed for exploration expenses incurred in Quebec until the end of 1996, subject to a 60-day grace period. Thus, in certain circumstances, surface mining exploration expenses incurred in Quebec may allow for a deduction equal to 175 per cent of these expenses. Moreover, in certain cases, a further exemption is granted with respect to the capital gain realized on the sale of flow-through shares, thereby enabling the holder to obtain tax breaks related to exploration.

Family Patrimony

As of July 1, 1989, married persons are required to take into consideration the rules adopted under Bill 146 with respect to economic equality between spouses in the event there is a partition of family patrimony, whether through separation from bed and board, dissolution or annulment of a marriage, or death.

These rules generally affect the partition of certain property between the spouses, not on the basis of individual property but on the net value of the property, by creating a right of claim between the spouses.

The property that is part of the partition is the family's principal and secondary residences, household furniture, motor vehicles used for family travel, and the benefits accrued during the marriage under public or private retirement plans. Any of the above-mentioned property that has been acquired before or during the marriage by way of succession, legacy, or gift is excluded from the family patrimony.

In the case of tax and estate planning, a spouse who makes a bequest to the other spouse should consider the implications of the partition of family patrimony. In addition to the bequest, the spouse will be entitled to 50 per cent of the net value of the property that is part of the family patrimony.

Corporations Operating in Quebec

Tax Rates. In Chapter 8, we discussed the tax as well as the planning advantages that are available through the incorporation of a business. It was mentioned that the tax structure varies depending on the province in which the income was earned, as well as on the type and amount of income.

Under Quebec legislation, the basic corporate rate is 16.25 per cent. However, active business income is subject to a tax reduction, the "small business deduction" (SBD). Thus, where a corporation claims the SBD in its federal tax return, a 10.5 per cent reduction is provided under the Quebec Taxation Act. However, where active business income is not subject to the federal SBD, a reduction of 7.35 per cent is provided.

The following schedule summarizes the effective Quebec corporate income tax rates:

	Active Business Income		
	Eligible for SBD	Not Eligible for SBD	Other Income
Basic rate	16.25%	16.25%	16.25%
Deduction allowed	10.50	7.35	—
Effective rate	5.75%	8.90%	16.25%

Exemptions for New Corporations. To stimulate the formation of new firms in Quebec, provincial legislation provides an income tax exemption to certain corporations. This tax exemption applies to the first three taxation years of new corporations with respect to active business income otherwise eligible for the small business deduction.

A corporation qualifies for the exemption in a taxation year if

- it was incorporated after May 1, 1986;
- it is not the result of an amalgamation;
- the year is one of its first three taxation years; and
- a tax return is filed within six months after the end of its first taxation year.

However, a corporation is not eligible for the exemption for the year if, among other things, it

- was associated with any other corporation;
- was not a "Canadian-controlled private corporation";
- carried on a personal services business; or
- carried on an eligible business as a member of a partnership.

Research and Development. To encourage research and development (R&D) in Quebec, provincial legislation provides several refundable tax credits to certain corporations that carry out R&D in the province.

The basic credit is 20 per cent of wages paid in Quebec for R&D activities in Quebec. If a corporation meets certain criteria and if the expenses are incurred pursuant to particular activities, the rate is increased to 40 per cent on the first $2 million of wages paid in Quebec for corporations whose assets are less than $25 million (this 40 per cent rate is progressively reduced to 20 per cent, on a linear basis, for corporations whose assets are more than $25 million and less than $50 million), and to 40 per cent of all R&D expenses incurred in Quebec pursuant to

- a university research contract with a prescribed public research centre;
- a pre-competitive research project;
- a catalyst project recognized by the government and certified by the Technological Development Fund, with the possibility of obtaining rents equal to 50 per cent of other eligible expenditures;
- an environmental technology innovation project that has received Technological Development Fund certification (with the possibility of grants equal to 40, 50, or 100 per cent of other eligible expenditures); or
- an R&D consortia project.

Training. To encourage corporations to provide training for their personnel, Quebec legislation provides refundable tax credits to all corporations for eligible training expenses incurred. An enhanced credit is available for certain small and medium-sized companies that do not have assets in excess of $25 million.

In general, eligible training expenses include training plans, costs incurred with an eligible training establishment, and, under certain conditions, wages paid to an employee during the training period, including travelling costs. Eligible expenses also include certain expenses incurred by corporations that agree to pay a part of the training costs of former employees and expenditures incurred for taking on student interns from professional-stream secondary schools or colleges, and certain types of apprentices.

The tax credit is 40 per cent of the expenditures incurred by small or medium-sized corporations. A 20 per cent credit is available for expenditures incurred by any other corporation.

Beginning January 1, 1996, the refundable training tax credit is replaced by a measure requiring employers whose payrolls exceed a certain amount during a reference period ($1 million in 1996; $500,000 in 1997; and $250,000 in 1998) to allocate 1 per cent of their payrolls to job training and manpower adjustment. Therefore, training expenditures currently eligible for the tax credit for on-the-job training are included in the expenditures that satisfy an employer's obligation. For employers who are not obliged to fulfil this requirement, the refundable manpower training tax credit is maintained through December 31, 1998.

CHAPTER TWELVE

Claiming Your GST and QST Rebates

Canadians must pay a 7 per cent Goods and Services Tax (GST) on most goods and services. In Quebec there is also a 6.5 per cent Quebec Sales Tax (QST).

The Basics

Only registrants are usually entitled to a rebate of the GST (and QST) paid. Because not all taxpayers can take advantage of the rebates, and to prevent some of those taxpayers being saddled with yet another expense for which no relief is available, certain individuals (e.g., employees and members of a partnership) may, under specific conditions, qualify for a rebate of the GST and QST paid, even if they are not registrants. These individuals may obtain this rebate (described below) by filing a special form with their income tax return. The rebate is available only for those expenses that are deductible when calculating income for income tax purposes. A rebate factor of 7/107 is used to calculate the qualifying portion of net expenses (6.5/106.5 for the QST rebate).

Taxpayers must remember to include the GST (or QST) rebate in the computation of their income for the taxation year in which the rebate is received. For example, such a rebate claimed in 1995, but received in 1996, must be included in the taxpayer's 1996 income.

Who May Claim a Rebate?

Only the employees of a registrant employer and the members of a registered partnership may claim the rebate, provided the registrants are not otherwise entitled to a rebate of the GST and QST on the same eligible expense.

For example, an employee of a non-profit organization is entitled to claim the rebate only if the organization is a registrant.

The most likely candidates for the rebate are commission and other salespeople, and employees and partners who have expenses related to a motor vehicle.

An employee cannot claim the GST rebate if his or her employer is a listed financial institution.

This means that a salesperson who works on commission at a brokerage firm or an insurance company is not eligible for the GST rebate on the expenses that he or she deducts when calculating income. This restriction does not apply to the QST rebate.

What Expenses Are Eligible?

The rebate is available solely for expenses deducted for income tax purposes in the computation of a taxpayer's employment income, or income from a partnership.

Some expenses that would normally be eligible for a rebate are entertainment expenses, advertising costs, professional membership dues, office expenses, leasing costs, various supplies, and automobile expenses such as capital cost allowance (CCA). The CCA deduction is allowed only if it applies to automobiles (and other motor vehicles), musical instruments, or aircraft.

For example, a rebate could not be claimed on the capital cost allowance of computer equipment. If the rebate is in respect of the capital cost of property, the rebate reduces the capital cost of the property at the time the rebate is received.

Note that expenses for which a reasonable allowance was paid by an employer are not eligible for a tax rebate. However, an employee or partner can claim a GST (or, in Quebec, a QST) rebate if the allowance received was unreasonable (i.e., one that must be included in the employee's or partner's income). In such cases, the employee or partner must obtain a statement from the employer or partnership to that effect.

A number of expenses deducted for income tax purposes are not eligible for a QST rebate – in particular, expenses related to an automobile (including operating expenses and depreciation, but excluding repairs and maintenance), telephone and other telecommunications services expenses, as well as entertainment expenses if the QST for these expenses was payable or has been paid before August 1, 1995. As of August 1, 1995, the restrictions on obtaining an input tax refund no longer apply. As a result, all employees and partners of a registered business, regardless of the business's amount of taxable supplies, can now claim a refund on this type of expense, provided that the QST was payable after July 31, 1995, and was not paid before August 1, 1995.

Filing an Application

In general, a rebate application (form GST370E, and form VD358 for the QST) is filed with the income tax return for the calendar year in which the expenses are incurred, although a claim can be made within four years after that calendar year. When computing the rebate, the consideration for an expense corresponds to the amount paid, which includes the amount of GST (or QST) paid. Partners can claim a GST or QST rebate using a calendar year, rather than the year-end of the partnership, if they deduct the expenses for income tax purposes on a calendar-year basis.

The following example illustrates how the GST and QST rebates are calculated.

Computing the Rebate

	Salesperson's Expenses	GST Rebate Computed on	QST Rebate Computed on
Entertainment	$800	$800	$500[1]
Office expenses:			
Electricity	400	400	100[1]
Property taxes	200	—	—
Insurance	300	—	—
Suppliers	100	100	100
Automobile expenses:			
CCA	1,000	1,000	1,000[1,2]
Interest	200	—	—
Insurance	400	—	—
Operating costs	150	150	75[1]
Repairs and maintenance	150	150	150
	$3,700	$2,600	$1,925

1 Expenses for which the QST was payable after July 31, 1995, and was not paid before August 1, 1995.
2 The CCA on the car is eligible for the QST rebate if the QST on the purchase of the car was payable after July 31, 1995, and was not paid before August 1, 1995. No QST rebate is available unless these conditions are met. Since the car in this example was purchased after July 31, 1995, the CCA qualifies for a rebate.

Notes:

1. The vendor is entitled to a GST rebate of $170 (7/107 of $2,600), and a QST rebate of $117 (6.5/106.5 of $1,925).
2. Since the property taxes, insurance, and interest are not subject to GST, no rebate is allowed. In Quebec, insurance is subject to the tax on insurance premiums, but does not give entitlement to a rebate.

3. The portion of the GST and QST rebates that relates to the expenses ($105 and $56, respectively) must be included in the income of the employee for income tax purposes, whereas another portion equal to $65 and $61, respectively, reduces the capital cost on which the CCA is based.
4. With the removal of the restrictions on the QST rebate, a rebate is available for the following expenses because the GST was payable after July 31, 1995, and was not paid before August 1, 1995: entertainment expenses, office expenses (electricity), and automobile expenses (CCA, operating expenses).

CHAPTER THIRTEEN

Facts and Figures for Calculating 1996 Taxes

PROVINCIAL RATES OF TAX FOR 1996 (%)[1]

Alberta[2, 3, 4]	45.5
British Columbia[3, 5]	52.0
Manitoba[2, 3, 6]	52.0
New Brunswick[3, 7]	64.0
Newfoundland[13]	69.0
Northwest Territories	45.0
Nova Scotia[2, 3, 8]	59.5
Ontario[2, 3, 9]	56.0
Prince Edward Island[3, 10]	59.5
Saskatchewan[2, 3, 11]	50.0
Yukon[3, 12]	50.0
Non-residents	52.0

Notes

1. Rates are expressed as a percentage of basic federal tax. The rates are those in effect at the date of publication.
2. There are tax reductions for lower levels of income in several provinces, including Alberta, Nova Scotia, Manitoba, Ontario, and Saskatchewan.
3. Surtaxes and flat tax not included.
4. Alberta levies a 0.5% flat tax on taxable income and an 8% surtax (not applicable on flat tax) on Alberta tax in excess of $3,500.

5. British Columbia imposes a 30% surtax on provincial tax in excess of $5,300 and an additional 20% surtax on provincial tax in excess of $9,000.
6. In Manitoba, a 2% flat tax is calculated on net income. As well, a 2% surtax is calculated on net income in excess of $30,000.
7. An 8% surtax applies to New Brunswick tax in excess of $13,500.
8. Nova Scotia imposes a 10% surtax on provincial tax in excess of $10,000.
9. The Ontario surtax (renamed the "Fair Share Health Care Levy") for 1996 is 20% on Ontario tax in excess of $5,310 plus 13% on Ontario tax in excess of $7,635.
10. Prince Edward Island imposes a 10% surtax on provincial tax in excess of $12,500.
11. Saskatchewan levies a 2% flat rate tax on net income. A 15% surtax applies to Saskatchewan tax (including the flat tax) in excess of $4,000. An additional 10% surtax applies to Saskatchewan basic tax plus the flat tax. For 1996, a $150 surtax reduction applies for individuals.
12. Yukon levies a 5% surtax on Yukon tax in excess of $6,000.
13. Newfoundland imposes a 10% surtax on provincial income tax in excess of $7,900.

FEDERAL RATES OF TAX FOR 1996[1]

Taxable Income	Tax	On Next
$0	$0 + 17%	$29,590
29,590	5,030 + 26	29,590
59,180	12,724 + 29	Excess

Note

1. Table does not incorporate the basic federal surtax of 3% nor the additional 5% surtax on federal tax in excess of $12,500.

FEDERAL RATES OF TAX FOR 1996 INCLUDING SURTAX

Taxable Income	Tax	On Next
$0	$0 + 17.51%	$29,590
29,590	4,051 + 26.78	29,590
59,180	11,975 + 29.87	3,015
62,195[1]	12,876 + 31.32	Excess

Note

1. The basic personal tax credit has been taken into account in determining the point at which the high-income surtax begins to apply since, unlike the basic rates (which are applied to taxable income), the surtax applies on tax. The credit has been deducted in calculating the amount of tax.

QUEBEC PERSONAL INCOME TAX MEASURES

1996 FEDERAL TAX – QUEBEC ONLY[1]

Taxable Income	Tax	On Next
$0	$0 + 14.71%	$29,590
29,590	3,402 + 22.49	29,590
59,180	10,057 + 25.09	3,015
62,195[2]	10,813 + 26.54	Excess

Notes

1. The rates take into account the federal surtax and the 16.5% federal tax abatement for residents of Quebec.
2. The basic personal tax credit has been taken into account in determining the point at which the high-income surtax begins to apply since, unlike the basic rates (which are applied to taxable income), the surtax applies on tax. The credit has been deducted in calculating the amount of tax.

1996 QUEBEC PROVINCIAL TAX

Taxable Income	Tax	On Next
$0	$0 + 16.0%	$ 7,000
7,000	1,120 + 19.0	7,000
14,000	2,450 + 21.0	9,000
23,000	4,340 + 23.0	27,000
50,000	10,550 + 24.0	Excess

Note

1. Table does not incorporate the 5% surtax on provincial tax in excess of $5,000, the additional 5% surtax on provincial tax in excess of $10,000, or the Quebec low-income reduction that applies at a rate of 2% of the excess of $10,000 over the amount of taxes payable after non-refundable tax credits. The above taxes payable reflect no non-refundable tax credits.

1996 QUEBEC PERSONAL TAX CREDITS

	Quebec Credit	Fed Tax Credit[1]
Basic	$1,180	$950
Person living alone[2]	210	0
Spouse[3]	1,180	791
Dependent children[4, 5]		
first child	520	0
each additional child	480	0
attending post-secondary school[6] – credit per term (max. 2 per year)	330	0
Single-parent family[5, 7]	260	0
Other dependants[5, 8]		
general	480	0
mentally or physically infirm	1,180	233

Quebec	Fed Tax Credit	Credit[1]
Age exemption[9]	440	512
Mentally or physically infirm[10]	440	623
Pension income [11]	200	147
Member of a religious order	792	0

Notes

1. Federal credits for Quebec residents are calculated on the assumption that the credit reduces the federal surtax (3%). The credit also reflects the 16.5% federal abatement.
2. The credit for an individual living alone is allowed to a single person who maintains a self-contained domestic establishment, or, if married, lives alone or with dependent children. The equivalent-to-spouse credit, which still exists for federal tax purposes, has been replaced in the Quebec system by a combination of the credits for the head of a single-parent family, the credit for the first dependent child, and the credit for a person living alone in a dwelling. Quebec also provides tax reductions for families in addition to these credits, eligibility for which is based on an income test.
3. In Quebec, this credit is reduced by 20% of the spouse's net income. The word "spouse" includes a common-law spouse. The federal tax credit is reduced by 17% of the spouse's net income exceeding $538.
4. Dependent children include: children, grandchildren, sisters, brothers, nieces, and nephews, under age 19 at the end of the year or over 18 and studying full-time.
5. For all Quebec credits claimed in respect of a dependant or a spouse, the income amount (i.e., the amount before the 20%

factor is applied) is reduced dollar for dollar by the dependant's or spouse's net income. Where the additional credits are claimed (e.g., post-secondary studies in addition to basic dependant claim or spouse credit plus transfer of credit for age 65 or over from a spouse), net income is deducted only once from the combined amounts. Federally, family allowance payments and the tax credits for dependent minor children have been replaced by a monthly payment, the Child Tax Benefit, usually paid to the mother. The payment is based on family income for earlier years, the number of children (more is paid for the third and each additional child), and their age (more is paid for each child under age seven). All children under age 18 qualify. The federal credits are indexed annually according to changes in the Consumer Price Index above 3%.

6. This additional credit is allowed when a dependant is in full-time attendance in a post-secondary educational program.
7. The credit for a single-parent family is available in respect of the first dependent child if the spouse credit is not claimed and the taxpayer does not live with a common-law spouse, is unmarried, or, if married, does not live with the spouse and is neither supported by nor supports that spouse. This credit may be claimed for one dependant only.
8. Other dependants include anyone over 18 years of age who is related to the taxpayer by blood, marriage, or adoption.
9. In 1995, the federal age tax credit is reduced by 15% of the taxpayer's net income exceeding $25,921. The Quebec tax system has not been harmonized with this federal measure. In certain circumstances, the age credit for taxpayers 65 and over may be transferred from a spouse. In this case, the transferred credit is not subject to the new reduction rules.
10. The disability credit may also be transferred in certain circumstances from a spouse and from other dependants.
11. Eligible pension income differs for persons age 65 and over, as compared to those under age 65. CPP/QPP benefits and OAS or GIS payments do not qualify, regardless of the taxpayer's age.

OTHER QUEBEC CREDITS AND DEDUCTIONS

Quebec pension plan and unemployment insurance contributions: 20% of contributions, up to specified limits.

Charitable donations: 20% of donations, not exceeding 20% of net income.

Health Services Fund contributions: 20% of contributions.

The Quebec tax credit for medical expenses is 20% (17% for federal tax purposes) in excess of the lesser of 3% of net income or $1,614.

For adults respecting the housing of a parent: a refundable tax credit of $550.

The deduction for tuition fees is maintained for Quebec tax purposes (instead of a credit). Moreover, tuition fees may not be transferred to another person for Quebec tax purposes.

1996 COMBINED FEDERAL AND PROVINCIAL PERSONAL INCOME TAX RATES [1, 6]

TAXABLE INCOME		Alberta[2, 3, 4] Prov. rate 45.5%		British Columbia[2] Prov. rate 52%		Manitoba[2, 3, 4] Prov. rate 52%	
From (A)	To (B)	Tax on (A)	Rate on Excess (B-A)	Tax on (A)	Rate on Excess (B-A)	Tax on (A)	Rate on Excess (B-A)
$0	$6,457	$0	0.00%	$0	0.00%	$0	0.00%
6,458	7,000	0	17.51%	0	26.35%	0	17.51%
7,001	7,132	95		143		95	
7,133	7,795	118		178		118	
7,796	8,347	234		352		234	30.35%
8,348	8,436	331		498		402	
8,437	8,538	346		521		429	
8,539	9,547	364		548		460	
9,548	9,573	541	29.86%	814		766	
9,574	10,000	549		821		774	
10,001	14,000	676		933		903	
14,001	15,000	1,871		1,987		2,117	
15,001	16,508	2,169		2,251		2,421	
16,509	18,999	2,620	25.75%	2,648		2,879	
19,000	19,513	3,261		3,305		3,635	
19,514	21,499	3,393		3,440		3,791	
21,500	23,000	3,905		3,963		4,393	28.35%
23,001	29,590	4,291		4,359		4,819	
29,591	30,000	5,987	39.11%	6,095	40.30%	6,687	42.30%
30,001	30,999	6,148		6,260		6,860	44.30%
31,000	39,203	6,538		6,663		7,303	
39,204	44,053	9,747		9,969		10,937	
44,054	50,000	11,644	40.06%	11,923		13,086	
50,001	50,936	14,026		14,320		15,720	
50,937	52,624	14,401		14,697		16,135	
52,625	53,667	15,077		15,378		16,883	
53,668	58,502	15,495		15,798	44.36%	17,345	
58,503	59,180	17,431		17,942		19,486	
59,181	60,469	17,704	44.62%	18,244	49.47%	19,788	48.95%
60,470	62,194	18,279		18,882		20,419	
62,195	66,103	19,049	46.07%	19,736	50.92%	21,263	50.40%
66,104	77,044	20,850		21,726		23,233	
77,045	78,771	25,890		27,298		28,748	
78,772	79,999	26,686		28,177	53.94%	29,618	
80,000	91,532	27,252		28,972	54.16%	30,237	
91,533	91,826	32,565		35,218		36,050	
91,827	and over	32,701		35,378		36,198	

TAXABLE INCOME		New Brunswick[2] Prov. rate 64%		Newfoundland Prov. rate 69%		Northwest Territories Rate 45%	
From (A)	To (B)	Tax on (A)	Rate on Excess (B-A)	Tax on (A)	Rate on Excess (B-A)	Tax on (A)	Rate on Excess (B-A)
$0	$6,457	$0	0.00%	$0	0.00%	$0	0.00%
6,458	7,000	0	28.39%	0	29.24%	0	25.16%
7,001	7,132	154		159		136	
7,133	7,795	191		197		170	
7,796	8,347	380		391		336	
8,348	8,436	536		552		475	
8,437	8,538	562		578		498	
8,539	9,547	590		608		523	
9,548	9,573	877		903		777	
9,574	10,000	884		911		784	
10,001	14,000	1,006		1,036		891	
14,001	15,000	2,141		2,205		1,898	
15,001	16,508	2,425		2,498		2,149	
16,509	18,999	2,853		2,939		2,529	
19,000	19,513	3,560		3,667		3,155	
19,514	21,499	3,706		3,817		3,285	
21,500	23,000	4,270		4,398		3,784	
23,001	29,590	4,696		4,837		4,162	
29,591	30,000	6,567	43.42%	6,763	44.72%	5,820	38.48%
30,001	30,999	6,745		6,947		5,978	
31,000	39,203	7,179		7,394		6,362	
39,204	44,053	10,741		11,062		9,519	
44,054	50,000	12,847		13,231		11,385	
50,001	50,936	15,429		15,891		13,674	
50,937	52,624	15,835		16,309		14,034	
52,625	53,667	16,568		17,064		14,683	
53,668	58,502	17,021		17,531		15,085	
58,503	59,180	19,120		19,693	46.51%	16,945	
59,181	60,469	19,416	48.43%	20,009	51.88%	17,207	42.92%
60,470	62,194	20,040		20,678		17,760	
62,195	66,103	20,875	49.88%	21,573	53.33%	18,500	44.37%
66,104	77,044	22,825		23,658		20,235	
77,045	78,771	28,283		29,493		25,089	
78,772	79,999	29,144		30,414		25,856	
80,000	91,532	29,757		31,069		26,401	
91,533	91,826	35,509		37,219		31,518	
91,827	and over	35,656	51.36%	37,376		31,648	

TAXABLE INCOME		Nova Scotia[2,3] Prov. rate 59.5%		Ontario[2,3] Prov. rate 56%		Prince Edward Island[2] Prov. rate 59.5%	
From (A)	To (B)	Tax on (A)	Rate on Excess (B-A)	Tax on (A)	Rate on Excess (B-A)	Tax on (A)	Rate on Excess (B-A)
$0	$6,457	$0	0.00%	$0	0.00%	$0	0.00%
6,458	7,000	0	17.51%	0	17.51%	0	27.63%
7,001	7,132	95		95		150	
7,133	7,795	118		118		186	
7,796	8,347	234		234		369	
8,348	8,436	331		331		522	
8,437	8,538	346	27.63%	346		546	
8,539	9,547	375		364	46.07%	575	
9,548	9,573	653		829		853	
9,574	10,000	661		841	27.03%	861	
10,001	14,000	779		957		979	
14,001	15,000	1,884		2,039		2,084	
15,001	16,508	2,160	32.63%	2,309		2,360	
16,509	18,999	2,652		2,717		2,776	
19,000	19,513	3,465	27.63%	3,390		3,465	
19,514	21,499	3,606		3,529		3,606	
21,500	23,000	4,155		4,066		4,155	
23,001	29,590	4,570		4,471		4,570	
29,591	30,000	6,390	42.25%	6,252	41.34%	6,390	42.25%
30,001	30,999	6,563		6,422		6,563	
31,000	39,203	6,985		6,835		6,985	
39,204	44,053	10,451		10,226		10,451	
44,054	50,000	12,500		12,231		12,500	
50,001	50,936	15,013		14,690		15,013	
50,937	52,624	15,408		15,077	44.25%	15,408	
52,625	53,667	16,122		15,824		16,122	
53,668	58,502	16,563		16,285		16,563	
58,503	59,180	18,605		18,425		18,605	
59,181	60,469	18,893	47.13%	18,726	49.36%	18,893	47.13%
60,470	62,194	19,500		19,362		19,500	
62,195	66,103	20,313	48.58%	20,214	50.81%	20,313	48.58%
66,104	77,044	22,212		22,200	52.92%	22,212	
77,045	78,771	27,526	50.30%	27,989		27,526	
78,772	79,999	28,395		28,904		28,365	
80,000	91,532	29,013		29,553		28,962	
91,533	91,826	34,814		35,657		34,564	50.30%
91,827	and over	34,962		35,812		34,712	

TAXABLE INCOME		Quebec[2,5] See page 185		Saskatchewan[2,3,4] Prov. rate 50%		Yukon[2] Rate 50%		Non-resident Rate 52%	
From (A)	To (B)	Tax on (A)	Rate on Excess (B-A)	Tax on (A)	Rate on Excess (B-A)	Tax on (A)	Rate on Excess (B-A)	Tax on (A)	Rate on Excess (B-A)
$0	$6,457	$0	0.00%	$0	0.00%	$0	0.00%	$0	0.00%
6,458	7,000	0	14.71%	0	17.51%	0	26.01%	0	26.35%
7,001	7,132	80		95		141		143	
7,133	7,795	99		118	28.01%	175		178	
7,796	8,347	197		304		348		352	
8,348	8,436	278	34.09%	458		491		498	
8,437	8,538	308		483		515		521	
8,539	9,547	343		512		541		548	
9,548	9,573	687		794		803		814	
9,574	10,000	696		802		810		821	
10,001	14,000	841		921	33.01%	921		933	
14,001	15,000	2,205	36.13%	2,242	28.01%	1,962		1,987	
15,001	16,508	2,566		2,522		2,222		2,251	
16,509	18,999	3,111		2,944		2,614		2,648	
19,000	19,513	4,011		3,642		3,262		3,305	
19,514	21,499	4,196		3,786	29.06%	3,396		3,440	
21,500	23,000	4,914		4,363		3,912		3,963	
23,001	29,590	5,456	38.16%	4,799		4,303		4,359	
29,591	30,000	7,971	45.95%	6,714	43.28%	6,016	39.78%	6,095	40.30%
30,001	30,999	8,159		6,891		6,179		6,260	
31,000	39,203	8,618	47.10%	7,324		6,577		6,663	
39,204	44,053	12,482		10,874	45.53%	9,840		9,969	
44,054	50,000	14,767		13,083		11,770		11,923	
50,001	50,936	17,568	48.17%	15,790		14,135		14,320	
50,937	52,624	18,018		16,216		14,508		14,697	
52,625	53,667	18,832	48.89%	16,985		15,179		15,378	
53,668	58,502	19,342		17,460		15,594		15,798	
58,503	59,180	21,705		19,661		17,517		17,746	
59,181	60,469	22,038	51.49%	19,971	50.50%	17,788	44.37%	18,021	44.95%
60,470	62,194	22,701		20,622		18,360	45.10%	18,600	
62,195	66,103	23,589	52.94%	21,493	51.95%	19,138	46.55%	19,375	46.40%
66,104	77,044	25,658		23,523		20,957		21,189	
77,045	78,771	31,450		29,207		26,050		26,266	
78,772	79,999	32,364		30,104		26,854		27,067	
80,000	91,532	33,014		30,742		27,425		27,637	
91,533	91,826	39,119		36,733		32,793		32,988	
91,827	and over	39,275		36,886		32,930		33,125	

Notes

1. Rates shown are marginal rates. At lower levels of taxable income, provincial low-income reductions, where applicable, distort this rate. Numbers have been rounded to the nearest dollar.
2. Provincial surtaxes apply as follows:

	Rate (%)	Application
Alberta	8	On Alberta tax (excluding flat tax) in excess of $3,500
British Columbia	30/50	30% on British Columbia tax in excess of $5,300 and an additional 20% on tax in excess of $9,000
Manitoba	2	Flat rate on net income in excess of $30,000
New Brunswick	8	On New Brunswick tax in excess of $13,500
Newfoundland	10	On Newfoundland tax in excess of $7,900
Nova Scotia	10	On Nova Scotia tax in excess of $10,000
Ontario	20/33	20% on Ontario tax between $5,310 and $7,635 and an additional 13% on tax in excess of $7,635
P.E.I.	10	On P.E.I. tax in excess of $12,500
Quebec	5/10	On Quebec tax in excess of $5,000 and $10,000, respectively
Saskatchewan	10/25	10% on Saskatchewan tax (including flat tax), less a $150 reduction for 1996, and an additional 15% on Saskatchewan tax (including flat tax) in excess of $4,000
Yukon	5	On Yukon tax in excess of $6,000

3. A low-income tax reduction applies. Reductions are phased out as income increases, which in certain cases results in an

increased marginal tax rate. The figures take into account only those reductions that apply to all taxpayers.

- The basic $200 Saskatchewan sales tax reduction (other reductions are based on family situation and age) eliminates provincial tax until taxable income reaches $7,133 to $10,000 and ceases to apply when taxable income reaches $14,000.
- The Alberta reduction eliminates provincial tax until taxable income reaches $9,545 and ceases when taxable income reaches $16,508.
- The Manitoba reduction eliminates provincial tax until taxable income reaches $7,793 and ceases to apply when taxable income reaches $21,500.
- The Nova Scotia reduction eliminates provincial tax until taxable income reaches $8,436 to $15,000 and ceases to apply when taxable income reaches $19,000.
- The Ontario reduction eliminates provincial tax until taxable income reaches $8,535 and ceases to apply when taxable income reaches $9,575.
- The Quebec reduction eliminates Quebec taxes payable up to taxable income of $8,347, but then applies at a rate of 2% of the excess of $10,000 over the amount of Quebec taxes payable (after non-refundable tax credits but before surtax) below $10,000. The reduction is completely eliminated at taxable income of $52,625. Quebec surtax continues to apply on basic Quebec tax before the low-income reduction.

4. A flat tax of 0.5% is applied to taxable income in Alberta. In Manitoba and Saskatchewan, a flat tax of 2% applies to net income. In the latter two cases, it is assumed that net income is equal to taxable income.
5. For purposes of comparison, it is assumed that taxable income for federal and Quebec purposes is the same. Taxpayers resident in Quebec receive a 16.5% abatement of federal tax.
6. Federal surtax is included in these rates and, in determining the brackets at which the rates apply, the federal personal tax credit of $1,098 has been taken into account.

MARGINAL TAX RATES FOR CAPITAL GAINS 1996[1]

Taxable Income	Alta.	B.C.	Man.	N.B.	Nfld.	N.W.T.
$21,501	19.31%	19.76%	21.26%	21.29%	21.93%	18.87%
23,001	19.31	19.76	21.26	21.29	21.93	18.87
29,591	29.33	30.23	31.73	32.57	33.54	28.86
30,001	29.33	30.23	33.23	32.57	33.54	28.86
31,000	29.33	30.23	33.23	32.57	33.54	28.86
39,205	29.33	30.23	33.23	32.57	33.54	28.86
44,053	30.04	30.23	33.23	32.57	33.54	28.86
50,001	30.04	30.23	33.23	32.57	33.54	28.86
50,938	30.04	30.23	33.23	32.57	33.54	28.86
52,625	30.04	30.23	33.23	32.57	33.54	28.86
53,669	30.04	33.27	33.23	32.57	33.54	28.86
58,503	30.04	33.27	33.23	32.57	34.89	28.86
59,181	33.47	37.11	36.71	36.32	38.91	32.19
60,471	33.47	37.11	36.71	36.32	38.91	32.19
62,195	34.55	38.19	37.80	37.41	40.00	33.28
66,105	34.55	38.19	37.80	37.41	40.00	33.28
77,045	34.55	38.19	37.80	37.41	40.00	33.28
78,773	34.55	40.46	37.80	37.41	40.00	33.28
80,000	34.55	40.62	37.80	37.41	40.00	33.28
91,534	34.55	40.62	37.80	37.41	40.00	33.28
91,828	34.55	40.62	37.80	38.52	40.00	33.28

Taxable Income	N.S.	Ont.	P.E.I.	Que.	Sask.	Yukon	Non-Res.
$21,501	20.72%	20.27%	20.72%	26.78%	21.80%	19.51%	19.76%
23,001	20.72	20.27	20.72	28.28	21.80	19.51	19.76
29,591	31.69	31.01	31.69	34.12	32.46	29.84	30.23
30,001	31.69	31.01	31.69	34.12	32.46	29.84	30.23
31,000	31.69	31.01	31.69	34.98	32.46	29.84	30.23
39,205	31.69	31.01	31.69	34.98	34.15	29.84	30.23
44,053	31.69	31.01	31.69	34.98	34.15	29.84	30.23
50,001	31.69	31.01	31.69	35.77	34.15	29.84	30.23
50,938	31.69	33.19	31.69	35.77	34.15	29.84	30.23
52,625	31.69	33.19	31.69	36.67	34.15	29.84	30.23
53,669	31.69	33.19	31.69	36.67	34.15	29.84	30.23
58,503	31.69	33.19	31.69	36.67	34.15	29.84	30.23
59,181	35.34	37.02	35.34	38.61	37.87	33.28	33.71
60,471	35.34	37.02	35.34	38.61	37.87	33.82	33.71
62,195	36.43	38.11	36.43	39.70	38.96	34.91	34.80
66,105	36.43	39.69	36.43	39.70	38.96	34.91	34.80
77,045	37.73	39.69	36.43	39.70	38.96	34.91	34.80
78,773	37.73	39.69	36.43	39.70	38.96	34.91	34.80
80,000	37.73	39.69	36.43	39.70	38.96	34.91	34.80
91,534	37.73	39.69	37.73	39.70	38.96	34.91	34.80
91,828	37.73	39.69	37.73	39.70	38.96	34.91	34.80

Note

1. Rates shown include surtaxes and flat rate taxes where applicable. Minimum tax considerations have been ignored. In deriving these rates, it was assumed that net income is equal to taxable income, that taxable income for Quebec purposes is the same as federal, and that only the basic personal tax credit applies ($1,098 federal, $1,180 Quebec). No provincial low-income reductions were taken into account in determining marginal rates.

MARGINAL TAX RATES FOR DIVIDENDS 1996[1]

Taxable Income	Alta.	B.C.	Man.	N.B.	Nfld.	N.W.T.
$21,501	7.43%	7.10%	9.60%	7.65%	7.88%	6.78%
23,001	7.43	7.10	9.60	7.65	7.88	6.78
29,591	24.14	24.54	27.04	26.44	27.23	23.43
30,001	24.14	24.54	29.54	26.44	27.23	23.43
31,000	24.14	24.54	29.54	26.44	27.23	23.43
39,205	24.14	24.54	29.54	26.44	27.23	23.43
44,053	24.71	24.54	29.54	26.44	27.23	23.43
50,001	24.71	24.54	29.54	26.44	27.23	23.43
50,938	24.71	24.54	29.54	26.44	27.23	23.43
52,625	24.71	24.54	29.54	26.44	27.23	23.43
53,669	24.71	27.01	29.54	26.44	27.23	23.43
58,503	24.71	27.01	29.54	26.44	28.33	23.43
59,181	30.42	33.41	35.35	32.70	35.03	28.98
60,471	30.42	33.41	35.35	32.70	35.03	28.98
62,195	31.40	34.39	36.33	33.68	36.01	29.96
66,105	31.40	34.39	36.33	33.68	36.01	29.96
77,045	31.40	34.39	36.33	33.68	36.01	29.96
78,773	31.40	36.43	36.33	33.68	36.01	29.96
80,000	31.40	36.57	36.33	33.68	36.01	29.96
91,534	31.40	36.57	36.33	33.68	36.01	29.96
91,828	31.40	36.57	36.33	34.69	36.01	29.96

Taxable Income	N.S.	Ont.	P.E.I.	Que.	Sask.	Yukon	Non-Res.
$21,501	7.45%	7.29%	7.45%	19.13%	9.99%	7.01%	7.10%
23,001	7.45	7.29	7.45	21.63	9.99	7.01	7.10
29,591	25.73	25.18	25.73	31.36	27.77	24.23	24.54
30,001	25.73	25.18	25.73	31.36	27.77	24.23	24.54
31,000	25.73	25.18	25.73	32.25	27.77	24.23	24.54
39,205	25.73	25.18	25.73	32.25	29.33	24.23	24.54
44,053	25.73	25.18	25.73	32.25	29.33	24.23	24.54
50,001	25.73	25.18	25.73	33.56	29.33	24.23	24.54
50,938	25.73	26.95	25.73	33.56	29.33	24.23	24.54
52,625	25.73	26.95	25.73	34.51	29.33	24.23	24.54
53,669	25.73	26.95	25.73	34.51	29.33	24.23	24.54
58,503	25.73	26.95	25.73	34.51	29.33	24.23	24.54
59,181	31.82	33.33	31.82	37.75	35.54	29.96	30.35
60,471	31.82	33.33	31.82	37.75	35.54	30.45	30.35
62,195	32.80	34.31	32.80	38.73	36.51	31.43	31.33
66,105	32.80	35.74	32.80	38.73	36.51	31.43	31.33
77,045	33.97	35.74	32.80	38.73	36.51	31.43	31.33
78,773	33.97	35.74	32.80	38.73	36.51	31.43	31.33
80,000	33.97	35.74	32.80	38.73	36.51	31.43	31.33
91,534	33.97	35.74	33.97	38.73	36.51	31.43	31.33
91,828	33.97	35.74	33.97	38.73	36.51	31.43	31.33

Note

1. Rates shown include surtaxes and flat rate taxes where applicable. Minimum tax considerations have been ignored. In deriving these rates, it was assumed that net income is equal to taxable income, that taxable income for Quebec purposes is the same as federal, and that only the basic personal tax credit applies ($1,098 federal, $1,180 Quebec). No provincial low-income reductions were taken into account in determining marginal rates.

PERSONAL TAX CREDITS FOR 1996 – COMBINED FEDERAL AND PROVINCIAL VALUE[1]

Personal tax credits are deductible in computing basic federal tax (the base for computing provincial tax). Note that on the T1 tax return you add up the income equivalent amounts (along with certain other items) and make a single conversion at 17% to arrive at your total tax credit. Since provincial tax is calculated as a percentage of your basic federal tax, the credit will also reduce your provincial tax liability. The combined amounts are shown for provinces other than Quebec.

Credits	Income Amount	Federal Credit	Alta 45.5%	B.C. 52.0%	Man. 52.0%	N.B. 64.0%
Basic	$6,456	$1,098	$1,725	$2,050	$1,756	$1,944
Spouse or equivalent[2, 3]	5,380	915	1,437	1,708	1,463	1,620
Other dependants[4]	1,583	269	423	503	431	477
Persons 65 or over[5]	3,482	592	930	1,105	947	1,048
Disability[5]	4,233	720	1,131	1,344	1,151	1,275

Credits	Nfld 69.0%	N.W.T. 45.0%	N.S. 59.5%	Ont. 56.0%	P.E.I. 59.5%	Sask. 50.0%	Yukon 50.0%
Basic	$2,018	$1,679	$1,904	$2,003	$1,904	$1,871	$1,762
Spouse or equivalent[2, 3]	1,682	1,399	1,586	1,669	1,586	1,559	1,468
Other dependants[4]	495	412	467	491	467	459	432
Persons 65 or over[5]	1,089	906	1,027	1,080	1,027	1,009	950
Disability[5]	1,323	1,101	1,248	1,313	1,248	1,227	1,155

Notes:

1. Credits are rounded to the nearest dollar. The combined amounts are based on provincial tax rates as shown and include the federal surtax of 8%. Provincial surtaxes are included at the highest applicable surtax rate. Note that credits do not affect flat taxes. The federal amounts exclude all surtaxes.
2. Common-law spouses are considered spouses for tax purposes. A common-law spouse is defined for tax purposes to be a person of the opposite sex with whom an individual is cohabiting in a conjugal relationship and has so cohabited for at least the preceding 12 months or, alternatively, a person with whom the individual cohabits in a conjugal relationship and shares a child.
3. The credit is reduced where the spouse's or the qualifying dependant's net income is between $538 and $5,918 and is eliminated if net income exceeds $5,918.
4. The credit is reduced if the dependant's income is between $2,690 and $4,273 and is eliminated when the dependant's income exceeds $4,273.
5. Where an individual is otherwise eligible for the tax credit, but is unable to use it, the credit may be transferred to a spouse. After 1994, an age credit for seniors with net incomes over $49,134 is no longer available.

Index

Deloitte & Touche Offices

National Offices

Toronto (150 King)	(416) 599-5399
Toronto (95 Wellington)	(416) 601-5650
Montréal	(514) 393-7115

British Columbia

Langley	(604) 534-7477
New Westminster	(604) 664-6200
Prince George	(250) 564-1111
Vancouver	(604) 669-4466
Victoria	(604) 360-5000

Alberta

Calgary	(403) 267-1700
Edmonton	(403) 421-3611

Saskatchewan

Regina	(306) 525-1600
Prince Albert / Saskatoon	(306) 763-7411
Saskatoon / Prince Albert	(306) 343-4400

Manitoba

Winnipeg	(204) 942-0051

Ontario

Cornwall	(613) 932-5421
Guelph	(519) 822-2000
Hamilton / St. Catharines	(905) 523-6770
Hawkesbury	(613) 632-4178
Kitchener	(519) 576-0880
London / Sarnia	(519) 679-1880
Mississauga	(905) 803-5100
Oshawa (905) 579-8202,	(905) 686-8249
Ottawa / Hull	(613) 236-2442
Sarnia / London	(519) 336-6133
St. Catharines / Hamilton	(905) 688-1841
Toronto	(416) 601-6150
Toronto North (North York & Markham)	(416) 229-2100
Windsor	(519) 258-8833

Québec
(Samson Bélair/Deloitte & Touche)

Alma	(418) 669-6969
Amos	(819) 732-8273
Baie-Comeau	(418) 589-5761
Chicoutimi	(418) 549-6650
Dolbeau	(418) 276-0133
Farnham	(514) 293-5327
Granby	(514) 372-3347
Grand-Mère	(819) 538-1721
Hull / Ottawa	(819) 770-3221
Jonquière	(418) 542-9523
La Baie (Ville De)	(418) 544-7313
La Malbaie	(418) 665-3965
Laval	(514) 978-3500
Longueuil	(514) 670-4270
Matane	(418) 566-2637
Montréal	(514) 393-7115
Québec	(418) 624-3333
Rimouski	(418) 724-4136
Roberval	(418) 275-2111
Rouyn-Noranda	(819) 762-0958
Saint-Hyacinthe	(514) 774-4000
Sept-Îles	(418) 968-1311
Shawinigan	(819) 537-7281
Sherbrooke	(819) 564-0384
St-Félicien	(418) 679-4711
Trois-Rivières	(819) 691-1212

New Brunswick

Fredericton	(506) 458-8105
Moncton	(506) 857-8400
Saint John	(506) 632-1080

Nova Scotia

Halifax	(902) 422-8541
Sydney	(902) 564-4517

Newfoundland

St. John's	(709) 576-8480